By the same author:

The Identity Society

Schools Without Failure

Reality Therapy

Mental Health or Mental Illness?

POSITIVE
ADDICTION

POSITIVE ADDICTION

William Glasser, M.D.

HARPER & ROW, PUBLISHERS
New York, Hagerstown, San Francisco, London

Designed by Janice Stern

Library of Congress Cataloging in Publication Data
Glasser, William, 1925–
    Positive addiction.

    Includes index.
    1. Self-actualization (Psychology) 2. Running—
Psychological aspects. 3. Transcendental medita-
tion. I. Title. [DNLM: 1. Psychology—Popular
works. BF145 G549p]
BF637.S4G55 1975   158'.1   75–15305
ISBN 0–06–011558–0

81 82 83 84 10

To my mother and father in the
sixtieth year of their marriage

contents

Acknowledgments

I would like to thank George Shuba for his willingness to discuss his possible positive addiction to swinging a bat. Thanks also to Ed Ford and Al Katz, two of my associates who sent me supporting material which helped me a great deal in developing the concept. I also appreciate the contribution of Robert Winquist, a vice-president of Mahareshi International University in Fairfield, Iowa, who devoted a great deal of time to exploring the ideas at several stages along the way. A special thanks to Joe Henderson, an addicted runner who edits *Runner's World,* whose cooperation provided me with essential material in Chapter Five. Thanks also to Steve Weggeland, who tabulated the several thousand questionnaires summarized in chapters Five and Six.

When the initial manuscript was finished, my wife, Naomi, spent a great deal of time reading it over and making a series of suggestions all of which made this a much better book. As usual, Hal Grove, my editor at Harper & Row, provided encouragement and help from start to finish.

POSITIVE
ADDICTION

one

STRENGTH—WHEN YOU HAVE IT
AND WHEN YOU DON'T

Very few of us realize how much we choose the misery in our lives. Even when we do, we still go ahead with the disastrous choice because we are convinced that we don't have the strength to choose better. A child doesn't give up in school, or a wife on her marriage, because each believes it's a good move. They give up because they no longer have the strength to keep up the struggle. I will first describe in detail how weakness is the cause of almost all the unfortunate choices we make. Then I will argue that anyone who wishes to become stronger seriously consider trying to become an addict.

If you accept the usual definition of addict, this is probably as far as you will read here because to you, and until recently to me, an addict is someone whose life is destroyed by heroin, alcohol, or gambling, and often the lives of those around him are ruined too. Smoking until you are short of breath and risking cancer, or eating until you are so obese you become repulsive to yourself and others, do not make you attractive. Everyone knows that too much coffee can make you nervous and sleepless, yet how many people can kick the coffee habit? I don't deny the truth in these common examples of addiction; but I do claim that addiction is not all bad. To the contrary, I believe there are a number of addictions that are as good as the above-named addictions are harmful. I call them *positive addictions because they strengthen us and make our lives more satisfying.* They exist in sharp contrast to the common or *negative addictions* like alcohol or heroin, which always weaken and often destroy us. While the concept is new, the practices I call positive addictions are not. They exist at present for thousands of people, a great number of whom are aware that they have a strong habit but few of whom think of themselves as addicted. Many of them are, however, and in this book I will call them positive addicts because, due to their addictions, they are almost always stronger than nonpositively addicted people who lead similar lives. With this added strength they live with more confidence, more creativity, and more happiness, and usually in much better health.

To begin let's examine what happens when we don't have enough strength to find the happiness that I believe most of us want more than anything else from our lives. There are those who would argue that just staying alive is the prime human need, but if we take a careful look at ourselves and those we know, that argument makes little sense. Certainly many people do cling to life when they are miserable and have almost no hope for happiness. They hang on, however, not because life itself is so rewarding but because of the old but accurate cliché, where there's life there's hope. If just staying alive were such an overpowering need, then suicide would be rare, which it is not. Each year at least fifty thousand people in the United States alone, most of whom are in good health, become convinced that there is no hope, no chance for fulfillment, pleasure, recognition, or whatever it is that most of us call happiness. They kill themselves because death seems preferable to the lives they are presently living. Besides suicide, there is also abortion which, wherever it is

2

legal, is now about as common as birth. I am not arguing the pros and cons of abortion, but I think in most cases when a mother decides to abort her child she does so because either her happiness or the happiness of her unborn child is at stake. It is a rare abortion today that takes place because the mother's life is in danger. Finally, although this is much less frequent because, unlike abortion, it is always illegal, mercy killing is motivated by the belief that there is more to living than just staying alive. These are powerful arguments that, for those strong enough to find them, fulfillment, pleasure, recognition, a sense of personal value, a sense of worth, the enjoyment of loving and being loved are not optional, they are the facts of life.

Each individual finds them in his or her own way, but in general everyone finds them through: (1) love—that is, through loving and being loved, and (2) by doing something one believes is worthwhile. From the time we are tiny we are told what is worthwhile and perhaps even more what is not. First by our parents, later by our teachers, employers, friends, ministers, neighbors, politicians, editors, we are bombarded with what we should and shouldn't do. We soon learn the pleasure of doing right and the pain of doing wrong. As we grow, we should learn to judge for ourselves what is worthwhile, but it takes a great deal of strength to do what is right when few people will agree with us for doing it. Most of us spend our lives in a series of compromises between doing what we believe in and doing what will please those who are important to us. Happiness depends a great deal on gaining enough strength to live with a minimum of these compromises. It is never as simple as when we are small, riding our two-wheeler and yelling, "Look, Ma, no hands . . ." or as totally accepted as an adult stepping on the surface of the moon, but no matter what it is, any accomplishment that gains some recognition brings us pleasure and the lack of accomplishment is always accompanied by pain. The recognition can be immediate or delayed. Sometimes we have to wait a long time for the payoff, but if we never get any recognition for accomplishment our lives are miserable. I need not discuss love because obviously it feels good when we have it and it hurts terribly when we don't.

To find the happiness we all desire we have to figure out: (1) what to do, (2) how to do it, and (3) *where to get the strength to get it done.* In the struggle for love and worth, what to do and how to do it are rarely difficult. If anything is possible, we usually have some idea of *what* could make us happy. Then coming up with some idea of *how* to do it is usually not that hard either. Even when we seem to be hung up on what to do or how to do it this hang-up is rarely the real problem. The problem is we don't have the *strength* to do what will make us happy. It is hard for us to admit to ourselves that we don't have what it takes so we tend to rationalize, to weep and wail about not knowing what to do or how to do it. As much as we may complain, we usually know that what we lack is not the know-how, but the strength.

As much as we need more strength, however, at some particular time in our lives we have a certain amount. For most of us there is no easy way to get more. If we had more strength we could have better lives, but we don't, so too many of us have to settle for less than we would like to have. When I say this I'm not talking only about the very weak who lead obviously miserable lives, I'm talking about almost everyone. Even people with considerable strength, when they look at their lives with candor, can usually see places where they settle for less. The simple statement we sometimes say out loud but more often say to ourselves, "The hell with it," means we are settling for less because we don't have it in us now to struggle for more. We settle for less with our marriages, our children, our employers or employees, and our neighbors than we know we should. We drink, smoke, and eat too much because it's easier than disciplining ourselves to say no. I am not recommending that we should be more rigid or contentious, for that too is weakness. It takes strength, however, to be warm, firm, humorous, and caring and still do what we know we ought to do. Our lives would be much better if we never said, "The hell with it!" This chapter is intended to explain in detail how people distort their lives to avoid the suffering that always accompanies the weakness that led us to give up and say, "The hell with it!"

There are times, not many but they do occur, when we really don't know what to do. Even here we are best off if we have the strength to face this fact, to find a way to give up gracefully rather than to thrash around accomplishing nothing. We continue a futile effort because we don't want to admit to ourselves that we don't have the strength to quit. We are stuck because it takes more guts than we have to change our ways. For example, we may hopelessly court someone who doesn't respond because we don't believe we have the strength to get someone else. It takes a lot of strength to risk getting rejected by someone new, so we hang onto the one we know and say, "The hell with it," because we are used to that pain. If we had more strength we would say not, "The hell with it," but *"The hell with all this pain,* I'll find someone else." Weak people carry a torch for life, they "enjoy" wallowing in their misery. They do so partly in the hope that someone will feel sorry for them and solve their problems and partly, as I will shortly explain, because they believe it hurts less this way.

It may not be easy to find love and worth but it is not that hard either. It can't be, because most people have the strength to find enough of both to be reasonably happy. There is, however, a large group of people in the world,

5

literally millions here in our own country, who don't have
enough strength and because they don't they are miserable.
Each morning millions of them get up knowing that today is
going to be a lousy, painful, miserable day. They may be
depressed, anxious, angry, sick, or crazy, or they may be
apathetic, but whatever they feel, behave, or think, they are
locked into pain and misery because they don't have the
strength to change their way of life. Since the obvious purpose of pain, misery, and suffering is to tell you something
is wrong, fix it, change it, reform, improve, get help; if you
don't have the strength to do it, you are stuck with the pain.
This is not to say that people with strength don't suffer—they
do. They have no immunity to life, but when they feel pain,
they get moving or at least they try to do something, and the
more strength they have the more successful their efforts
are. There are lots of times, however, when there is nothing
they can do. When this happens, as it does to all of us, those
with strength just bear the pain while they figure out what to
do. They prefer to suffer rather than do something irrational
that might kill their chances ever to find happiness. Strong
people wait a lot; they have discovered that time does heal
many wounds.

In between the very strong, who are mostly happy, and the
miserably weak are the partially strong or the almost strong
enough. It is here that most of us exist, strong enough to get
along fairly well but not strong enough to live without a lot
of unnecessary suffering. It is mostly to this majority group
in our society that this book is aimed. Many of us are far from
inadequate but we are not strong enough to handle every
part of a complex life adequately. We may have ample love
but lose our jobs and fall apart, or we may have good jobs
but get rejected in our private lives. If we haven't enough
strength we attempt to reduce our suffering by partially giving up. We never throw the sponge in altogether but we tend

to give up in part, to try to reduce pain that always comes when we can't get the job done. For example, a while back I worked voluntarily for four years in a very tough situation and every afternoon my head hurt. I don't consider myself weak, but part of me was saying, "Give up, don't suffer the problems of this miserable job." Another part of me was saying, "Hang in there." The part of me that wanted to give up was trying to make its point by causing my head to hurt so I could better rationalize a decision to quit. I was either too strong or too stupid to quit but not so strong that I could do the job without headaches. When I finished the job with some success the headaches went away.

Let's discuss this whole concept of how misery leads to giving up. We will discuss it as though the person gives up completely, as many weak people do, but even more of us do so partly. The process, however, is exactly the same, only the degree differs. In any case, the best solution for all of us, weak or strong, is to get stronger. Too many of us are not in the fortunate position of being able to finish the job and get rid of the headaches.

GIVING UP—
THE FIRST CHOICE OF THE WEAK

What happens if you don't have the strength to begin to deal with the pain adequately? For the millions of people who don't, life is like having a toothache with no money to see a dentist. It doesn't hurt any less because you can't afford dental care—if anything it hurts more. In desperate attempts to get rid of pain, people without sufficient strength are driven to a choice that most of us with adequate strength never seriously contemplate. They choose to give up, a choice they feel forced to make because they don't believe

7

anything else will relieve the pain of their situation. I am sure that to many people reading this book giving up is not a viable option. How can anyone even contemplate giving up when his only chance for happiness is to keep struggling for what he doesn't have: sufficient love and worth? Some give up completely and more give up partly, not because they don't want happiness—they want it as much as anyone else. They give up because at this miserable point in their lives, happiness is not even on their minds. What is on their minds is the hope that through giving up they will get relief from the constant misery of not having and of believing they probably never will have what they need. If you were convinced, and believe me millions are, that continuing to try would result only in further failure, then after suffering your limit, it is likely you would conclude, "Why keep struggling? I won't make it anyway." The reason so many people give up is not that they want to accept lives of misery. They give up because it hurts more to keep trying when the effort always fails. These people are weak. They have already accepted the fact that life will be miserable; what's on their minds is a way to make it less miserable. Just because the fox said the grapes were sour didn't make them sour. What made them sour was the fact that he couldn't reach them. It hurt less to stop jumping. If, however, another friendly but more agile fox had offered him a bunch of delicious grapes to prove to him that the grapes were good, he probably would have called him a troublemaker and avoided him. Most people who give up tend to stay away from people who succeed. After all, what player who barely breaks 100 wants to play golf regularly with someone who shoots par, no matter how charming he is?

Sisyphus, the Greek giant who aspired to be a god, was, for his presumption, doomed by the gods to eternal punishment. He was forced to push a large boulder up a mountain and just before the boulder reached the top of the mountain, as he was about to set it in place, a god would reach out and flick it all the way back down the mountain. Sisyphus then had to walk back down and start pushing the boulder up again, to do this each day for eternity. Many people believe themselves to be in much the same position. It seems to them that to find something worthwhile to do with their lives or to find someone who really cares about them is impossible, so why keep trying? Unlike Sisyphus, who was cursed by the gods so he couldn't quit, if you and I pushed the boulder up a mountain once or twice only to have it flicked down, we would say, "The hell with it, we quit." We quit because the pain of attempting to find happiness and not finding it hurts much more than giving up. I maintain that almost everyone in the Western World who makes the first choice of the weak, the choice to give up, makes it on the basis that he hasn't the strength to keep trying. This doesn't mean everyone gives up in the same way or by the same amount; there are certainly variations in what people do. Only a few give up completely but huge numbers settle for a lot less love or worth in their lives than they could have if they had the strength to work for more.

They don't look at it that way. Their last concern is getting more, their first concern is hurting less. They may not be totally miserable but they are miserable enough and they want to hurt less. They may in some cases seem hardly to hurt at all, but we should keep in mind that we can never feel another person's pain. They may even know how much happier they would be if they took a chance and tried for more, but they don't believe they have the strength to succeed. Furthermore, because they are weak they tend to blot out of their minds what they might do to get stronger; they settle for a minimal life because they haven't the strength for a better one.

I am sure that as you read these first paragraphs and on into the symptom choices that follow, you may recognize yourself in many places. While you may not give up completely, there are many times when, lacking strength, you settle for less or choose a symptom, as I chose headaches. Perhaps the beginning of gaining strength is becoming aware of the bad choices you make. Just knowing that you choose much of your misery yourself will help you get the idea that it may be worth trying to make a better choice. If you believe your misery just happens to you and you have no control over it, then you will never get much more than what you are getting now from life. But there is a fact of life that keeps many of us from recognizing that we choose a lot of our misery. That fact is that for many of us the world we live in is miserable. If you argue that the world may be responsible for a great deal of our inability to make the right choices with our lives you have a lot of truth behind your argument.

For example, how can a child possibly gain the strength to succeed in school if he can't speak English or if his teacher is prejudiced against him or if he never gets breakfast and his stomach hurts so much that he can't concentrate? Is it his fault if he chooses to give up? Isn't it the fault of the system that denies him the chance to fulfill his needs? Isn't the system, for him, much like the curse of Sisyphus in that he must stay in school for ten to twelve years knowing he will never even get close to success? Of course, much human suffering is the system's fault. Of course, everyone in the world should be given a fighting chance for love and worth, and should be raised in a way that gives him or her the strength to fight for a fair share, but the facts are that the world is not the way many of us would like it to be. Therefore, while I believe it is the responsibility of strong people all over to work hard to make the world better, until they do, it remains the task of all of us, weak or strong, to do the best we can for ourselves.

To tell a weak or inadequate person, as many well-meaning but misdirected social scientists and politicians do, that he isn't responsible for his misery because the world he lives in denies him a chance may be true. In practice, however, it only locks him further into weakness, into choosing to give up and then rationalizing, perhaps more accurately than the fox, that his world is sour. My job, as a psychiatrist and educator, is to try to help the weak grow stronger regardless of their situation. As a citizen I try to make the world better —that is my ongoing responsibility (it's yours, too). *But the thesis of this book is that many people, weak and strong, can help themselves to be stronger, and an important new path to strength may be positive addiction.* If more of us gain strength maybe we will make a better world; there is little chance we will do so if too many of us are weak.

THE SYMPTOM CATEGORIES— THE SECOND CHOICE OF THE WEAK

Perhaps the best way to demonstrate what usually happens when someone, after giving up, decides to make the second choice is to join me in my office where I am seeing such a person for the first time. Ordinarily I start the conversation saying something like, "Well, tell me a little bit about the difficulty" or "What's the problem?" or "What do you think is wrong?" Quite frequently he will look at me and very clearly, very calmly, and very pointedly say he is here because he is depressed. For him the first choice in dealing with life's problems—to give up—is no longer satisfactory; the pain has returned and in a further attempt to reduce his suffering he has made one of the common second choices—to become depressed. Depression is no mystery. Everyone reading this book knows exactly what it is. We have all experienced at least mild episodes of depression many times in our lives, but when a person tells a psychiatrist that he is depressed, it is always serious. Even though he doesn't actually speak the words, I assume he is saying much more. "Dr. Glasser, I am depressed and I have come to see you because I want you, as a psychiatrist, to help me get over the painful, miserable way I feel." So with that he throws the ball to me. I have been in practice quite a while but this is always a tense moment because I know he expects that somehow or other I will quickly help him to get rid of his pain. Regardless of what may have caused the depression, his fault or not, what is real to him is what he feels, and *he hurts*. He is on a hot stove and can't seem to get off. He is saying, "I have made a great effort to come here to your office [and for a depressed person that is a pretty big effort for which he may even want a little recognition] and I want something done by you to rid me of this misery now." The problem is that, right then, there is nothing I can do. I have no magic wand to dispel his pain. Sometimes, if I feel a great deal of pressure, I become facetious and say in a joking way, "I'll tell you what, cheer up!" Now when I tell what I have just written here to an audience, they always laugh; but why does it strike them so funny? What's so wrong with my advice? The man said he was upset, depressed, and miserable; he is seeking help *now,* so I say, "Cheer up, stop hurting!"

People laugh because they recognize the futility of that simplistic advice. We have all been depressed and been told by some well-meaning fool to cheer up, a bit of advice that strikes us at the time as about as helpful as bailing out the *Titanic* with a teacup. Sometimes the client takes me seriously for a moment and says, "What do you mean, cheer up? Didn't you hear me, I just told you that I am depressed. If I could cheer up, my God, I would! The problem is I can't, that's why I am here." What he is saying is true, but why doesn't he cheer up? Why does he cling so tenaciously to his misery? He clings to it, I believe, because, as miserable as he is, his depression has some value to him. As he sits in my office he isn't aware of this—he thinks his depression is the worst thing that has ever happened to him. What I contend is that he won't give up his depression because he believes, even though he isn't aware of this belief, that if he drops his depression, he will hurt more than if he keeps it. As painful as his choice of depression is, it, like all the second choices, is less painful than the first choice of giving up.

All seriously depressed people (and many others whom I'll discuss shortly) choose one of four categories of symptoms very soon after they make the first choice. They had given up to reduce the severe pain of trying unsuccessfully to gain love and worth. Unfortunately, when you give up, while it was reduced for a while, the pain tends to return because you can't give up permanently on what you need for happiness without suffering. It may not hurt as much but it still hurts plenty, so this client and countless other people look around for something to reduce the pain again, and in the client's case, although like all those who make a second choice he is totally unaware that it *is* a choice, he chose depression. Depression is an extremely common choice, perhaps the most common symptom of all, but why does it reduce the pain?

Let me explain. Suppose the client says, "Dr. Glasser, look, I can't cheer up; my wife left me suddenly and moved in with someone else." He is trying to explain how terribly he has been put down, to make it clear why he can't cheer up. My answer would never be, though at times I must admit I am tempted, to tell him to go out and find another woman. He's had enough of that advice from his friends. He may anticipate my temptation by saying, "Please doctor, don't tell me to find someone else. Who'd be interested in me the way I am now?" He blames his inadequacy, his giving up, his immobility, and as we talk further most of his problems center on his depression. He has not the vaguest idea that he has *chosen* to be depressed. He doesn't realize that to a great extent the depression allows him to rationalize his problem. He doesn't realize that now he need not face his inadequacy because in his eyes he isn't inadequate, he is "sick." Painful as it is, the depression he has chosen is to him less painful than facing his inadequacy, his giving up. With the first choice, giving up, he relinquished responsibility, but with the second choice, depression, he is now shielded from his inadequacy and able to turn to others. Like the fox he may call the grapes sour, but the main point is that since he isn't going to jump for them anymore anyway, he has a perfect excuse: Who can jump when he is so depressed? Furthermore, he is now in a better position to ask for help because almost no one holds a depressed man responsible for his misery. He may even reject help because he worries that if he does accept help he may eventually have to help himself. So what he does is to complain a lot, but hurt less, because his depression is now the protector of his inadequacy. His own feelings, painful as they may be, have become his friend.

He clings to depression because now the depression substitutes for the love and worth he is convinced he can no longer get in the real world. It may not be a good substitute but it's the best he has. To repeat, he becomes involved with it because, first, it rationalizes his quitting position and makes him more acceptable to himself. Second, it puts him in a position to ask for help, to try to get someone to do for him what he hasn't been able to do for himself. When he gave up, people tended to turn away from him as a quitter, but now that he is suffering, when he asks for help, when he says, "Pay attention to my obvious misery," it is likely someone will. It is common for him to test their concern by saying, "Leave me alone" in order to check out how much they really care. In my office, however, cooperative or not, he wants to be taken care of or at least to get some attention. He hasn't the strength to buckle down and help himself; if he had, he would not be depressed. Even an expert may fall into the trap of attempting to help him rather than helping him to help himself. His friends and family usually do and I plead guilty on more than one occasion myself. He needs me, and no matter how many rejection games he plays I shouldn't reject him, but I shouldn't claim I can do very much for him either. I point out gently but firmly after we have made friends that he must help himself and I work with him to make a plan to do so. If he does help himself, then he will no longer need his depression, which right now he believes is his only "friend." If all he comes to my office for is to check out what I can offer and then reject it, he will pay a dear price in pain and misery. Most of us have paid this price on more than one occasion but not so often or for as long as those who see psychiatrists for depression.

With this example in mind, let's take a look at the chart below showing the four symptom categories—one or more of which are frequent second choices of the weak.

THE SECOND CHOICES OF THE WEAK

THE FOUR MAJOR SYMPTOM CATEGORIES	EXAMPLES OF COMMON SYMPTOMS
1. To act out	tantrums, delinquency, crime, sociopathic and psychopathic behavior
2. To become involved with your own emotions	depressed, fearful, phobic, tense, anxious, sad, dejected, bitchy, griping, haughty, snide, angry, hysterical, suspicious
3. To become crazy	psychotic, paranoid, hallucinating, delusional, conversion reaction
4. Psychosomatic	headaches, neckaches, backaches, sinus trouble, migraine, hypertension, heart disease, asthma, many allergies, duodenal ulcers, ileitis, colitis, chronic diarrhea, urinary urgency, arthritis

Although I will discuss these second choices as full-blown symptoms, almost all of us suffer mildly from one or more of them from time to time. When we say, "The hell with it," many of us then choose category one to act out briefly in angry, irrational ways. We all experience temporary episodes of painful depression, tension, fears, and anxiety, category two. Few of us are exempt from an occasional "crazy" thought, and most of us suffer on and off from aches, pains, or mild chronic illnesses that don't respond to medical treatment, categories three and four. We would have to have superhuman strength never to choose a symptom when we are temporarily frustrated or rejected, but the stronger we are the less we suffer from the choice.

Acting out, the first symptom category, is seen most often in children. When a little child is frustrated, when he doesn't get the attention he wants, he often has a tantrum. He screams, yells, and cries because he has learned as a baby that if he creates a fuss, someone will attempt to solve his problem for him. As he grows older, if no one stops him, he usually moves from tantrums into incorrigible behavior. By his teenage years he fits into that huge catch-all group we call juvenile delinquents. He behaves as if what he wants is all that counts; the rules and regulations that apply to us don't apply to him. Many adults continue in these ways—they become criminals, con men, psychopaths, behaving the way they want in an attempt to gain some power and recognition which may reduce the pain of their empty lives. Sometimes the behavior succeeds. They are able to break the rules successfully. This reinforces their choice; they become even more involved with themselves. They frequently become exhilarated with their own twisted success when things go their way. This adds to their rationalization that "straight" people are fools, chumps, or mooches, as they are known to the men who con them. Most sociopathic people tend to get overconfident and disdainful of others while their behavior is working. They push those around them more and more until, sometimes, they get stopped by a court of law. While many of us never go so far as to wind up before a judge, still there are few of us—adults or children—doing only what we want, legal or illegal, who are able to continue indefinitely. Eventually our behavior may grow wild and self-destructive. Many a parent has seen his child in this situation, and unless the child is stopped he may destroy himself or someone else. Whether he is a child acting up at home or in school, a delinquent on the streets, or an adult writing a lot of bad checks or robbing banks, sooner or later someone will say, "Stop," or "Go away," or "We don't give a damn," and the behavior no longer works. When his behavior doesn't work, especially if he is a criminal being locked up, or if not a criminal, he is being totally rejected, the pain starts again. If he is in prison, he ends up in smaller and smaller rooms until he is finally immobilized in a straitjacket. We may criticize the prison officials who lock him up but he truly may be uncontrollable; the pain drives him into this behavior because he believes only acting out will reduce his pain. When parents call me, desperate because of a totally out-of-control child, the only advice I can give them is to control him, which usually means employing juvenile corrections. Nothing else will work. If he can be controlled through probation or other legal means, then he may be able to be helped by a good probation officer or a therapist; but to be helped, first he must be stopped. Only then has he a chance to slow down and to think seriously about how poor his choice to act out is, how it locks him away from love and worth. Although there is no shortage of people who act out, most of us stop after childhood. We learn early from firm parents or teachers that tantrums won't work for us. Our advisers may stop our acting out, but if they don't help us to learn how to find love and worth we are likely to choose another symptom category, usually to become involved with one of our own emotions, as did the depressed man who came to my office.

As I said, depression, as well as acting out, happens to all of us for brief periods when we lack love and worth. The stronger we are the less it will happen, but people who have given up often become deeply involved not only with depression but also with anxiety, fear, tension, dejection, apathy, or some self-selected emotion that is a personal hybrid of these common feelings. Emotions are chosen, especially fear or depression, because they are safer than acting out. Acting out, when it works, gets rid of a lot more pain, but it hurts terribly when it is stopped, so most of us don't try it very long. Early in life we learn to become involved with our own emotions, which may upset the people who care for us but it doesn't alienate them, at least not for a long time, sometimes never. It is amazing how many people will stick by a depressed relative or friend for a lifetime, usually and unfortunately, in a kind of misery symbiosis. But when we learn to become fearful and anxious, upset, dejected, it is our feelings that become, to us, our true friends. They protect us from our inadequacy and replace our human friends and family. Since the second symptom category is almost always so uncomfortable, so painful, seemingly so alien to our welfare, throughout almost the whole history of psychiatry it has been difficult for most psychiatrists to accept that depression is a choice. Many experts in my field behave as if it came from the outside, beyond the patient's control, that he "caught it" as if it were some sort of psychiatric chicken pox. I believe this position is wrong. *Depression, no more than acting out, does not come from the outside. We don't catch it like chicken pox. It is out of our weakness that we choose to be depressed because we have discovered that not making this choice is even more painful.* Reducing pain is the whole purpose of the second choice. If the first choice reduced it enough we would stop there. Some people, especially apathetic schoolchildren, do.

3) The third symptom category is the choice to become crazy, psychotic, nuts, loony, bonkers, schizophrenic. There are a dozen popular, as well as pseudoscientific, words for this condition. I happen to prefer "crazy" because it is understandable; it doesn't have the pseudoscientific connotation of schizophrenia, it is not technical, and it emphasizes much better than any of the other terms *the choice aspect* of this

category. Schizophrenia sounds so much like a disease that prominent scientists delude themselves into searching for its cure, when the "cure" is within each crazy person who has chosen it. If he can find love or worth he will give up the choice readily—a big "if," I will admit, but hundreds do each day as they are discharged from good hospitals and clinics. With adequate treatment they learn to become strong enough to stop choosing to be crazy. Becoming crazy is actually a fairly sensible choice for the weak because no one expects a crazy person to fulfill his needs in the real world for the obvious reason that he is no longer in it. He now lives in the world of his own mind, and there within his own mind, crazy as it may be, he tries to find, and to some extent usually succeeds in finding, a substitute for the adequacy he can't find in reality. Within his own mind, within his own imagination, out of his own thought processes, he may be able to reduce the pain of his failure and find a little relief. For inadequacy he provides delusions of grandeur, for loneliness hallucinations to keep him company. He may have a delusion that everybody loves him or that he is an overwhelmingly omnipotent person, which does relieve his pain. Every mental hospital has one or two Jesus Christs, the acme of omnipotence and power. When all of this is created within a person's own mind we call it crazy, but it makes sense to him because it doesn't hurt as much as being lucid but miserably inadequate.

Most people with psychosis, however, withdraw only partially. They are not willing to withdraw totally into their own minds and lose the real world altogether, a step that is reported by ex-crazy people as very painful. To the degree they won't or can't accept total insanity they continue to suffer the pain of inadequacy, so they are really caught in the middle, actually a very common place for them to be. If they give up enough reality they may be committed to hospitals in which they lose their freedom. Too often they are subjected to barbaric treatment with no one to protect them from it, treatment like excessive electric shock or lobotomy. Even if they are treated well, to be locked up is a reality that compounds their pain. My experience as a psychiatrist has shown me that most of the people who are crazy are far from completely comfortable with their craziness and in an attempt to relieve their discomfort they may also follow the other symptom pathways. They may act out with aggressive behavior or they may be anxious or depressed. There is no rule that says we must choose only one symptom; many people often choose several but usually one predominates. Interestingly enough, fifty years ago more people used to choose craziness than acting out, but now many more people choose the first symptom category, acting out. This reversal of symptom choices (the pain is the same) has come about because our world promotes this choice through movies and television, which glorify sociopaths. Because we also allow so much more aberrant behavior that used to be taboo to go on in our society, fewer and fewer people choose to withdraw from the real world because of societal pressure.

In the beginning, when they are contemplating the choice to become crazy, most people are very anxious. It is upsetting to withdraw from the world into your own mind, to give up on others and settle for yourself. When they are tentatively choosing, they report flashes, brief feelings of unreality, all of which they have chosen, but they don't recognize the choice. They are testing out their choice and reporting on the test, perhaps, as a way to get help. They believe the voices are really coming from outside because that's what it sounds like, but the human brain is perfectly capable of creating a sound within itself. As one listens to his hallucinations, his own self-created sounds, they are very convincing. Working with a hallucinating patient it almost seems as though, if

21

you strained your ears, you would hear his voices too. What this proves, however, is that people do get deeply involved with their own personal craziness and if it is convincing to their doctors it certainly would be convincing to them. Always in the beginning and often later this is their way of saying, "Help me to be stronger, I can't make it. Please help me to stop choosing craziness, help me to live in the real world." And a good hospital ward, such as Dr. G. L. Harrington ran in the Los Angeles VA Hospital, can do just that. (See *Reality Therapy,* Chapter Four.)

The final symptom category is the choice to have a physical symptom or go further and become physically ill in an attempt to reduce the pain of the first choice, giving up. Millions of people suffer from this very popular choice of a psychosomatic illness, an illness caused by their inability to gain love and worth. Miserable as the sickness is, it is not as painful as the inadequacy. The variety of psychosomatic illnesses is myriad. William Osler, the famous physician who practiced around the turn of the century, stated, and I only paraphrase here, that there is no disease known to man that cannot be imitated so well by a psychosomatic condition that even a good doctor will be unable to tell whether the symptoms come from within or without.

For example, you may go to a doctor with severe headaches and ask for help—the pain is killing you. But if the severe headaches are caused by your inadequacy and are a way to rationalize failure or lack of sufficient strength, what can the doctor do medically? Of course, he can and should check you carefully, but if there is no medical cause he won't find anything, so all he can ordinarily do is give you medicine to relieve the pain. Since aspirin is the best pain reliever we have for nonpsychosomatic pain, if aspirin doesn't work, it's an important clue that we are dealing with a psychosomatic choice. Most headaches, even severe migraines, have no known organic cause, no known physical reason for the person to cause the blood vessels on one side of his head to constrict, but he can do it. How the lack of love and worth can lead to this is not known, but it is well known that when the person gains more strength the headaches go. As I described earlier, almost all of us have headaches, usually when we are under stress and lack sufficient strength, but most of us pull ourselves together, relax, and the headaches disappear. Yet people who are failures often have chronic headaches day after day, year after year, "incapacitating" the person. I put incapacitating in quotes because the incapacity really causes the headaches, even though with the suffering it so much seems the other way around. As in the other symptom choices the symptom masks the inadequacy, but psychosomatic illnesses such as headaches are a good choice because they obviously allow the sufferer to ask for help. Unfortunately, the help he asks for is the relief of the pain of the headaches, which is not nearly all the help he needs. Few doctors will say, "Look, your headaches are caused by inadequacy; take some aspirin and then go and find some more love and do something more worthwhile." Doctors find it very difficult to make these suggestions, not because they don't recognize the psychosomatic cause of the symptom. Many do. They don't confront the patient because they don't want the abuse they will get from a person whose whole purpose for having the headaches is to rationalize his long-term inability to find love and worth. Even if the doctor does confront him and the patient is cooperative he may only say, "You are right, 'doc,' but really what can I do with these headaches?" Besides, for a weak person, love and worth are not that easy to find, but with good counseling at least he may have a chance. Medical treatment will be ineffective or worse because it tends to lock the symptom in.

It has become a vicious circle in our society. Doctors'

23

offices are increasingly clogged with patients with psychosomatic complaints being treated medically for their symptoms, usually with drugs. The more this occurs the less likely
they are to face their inadequacies and the more their heads
hurt when the drug wears off. Even if the doctor does say,
"Get going" and the patient is not dependent on drugs and
is willing to try, he needs more direction than a brief bit of
advice. He needs to go where he can get some help to increase his strength or he must learn to do it on his own. Both
of these are hard; they take time, but if they aren't suggested,
the doctor, by standing pat, inadvertently adds his weight to
the view that the patient is physically ill, rather than inadequate. Obviously the doctor's role is critical and his job is not
easy. Just a suggestion that the trouble is psychosomatic
may cause the patient to run to another doctor. To make the
proper suggestion takes time and patience and, unfortunately, many doctors don't have the time.

While I have used headaches as an example, there are
other psychosomatic symptoms and illnesses. Backache, for
example, is now America's number one complaint. Pain in
the lower back, usually radiating down one leg, may be
caused by a slipped disc, but this cause, even when reme-
died, will not stop the pain if it is psychosomatic. It seems like
such a good cause-and-effect situation that many doctors are
fooled into overtreatment, again compounding the difficulty.
Something wrong with the back and back pain don't necessarily correlate. While they can coexist, inadequacy is more
likely the major cause of most back pain even though most
people in our sedentary society have far from perfect backs.
On the other hand, I have seen people whose backs are so
distorted that you feel uncomfortable looking at them, but
because they are adequate they have no pain. One man
walked around the VA hospital where I interned proudly car-
rying an X ray showing his lumbar spine curved like an *S* but

24

he had no pain or discomfort whatsoever. He had a bad back but a strong head.

I have seen men with muscular physiques doubled up with excruciating back pain, examined by doctor after doctor, none of whom could find any physical cause for the pain. To rationalize their inadequacies these "strong" men often push their doctors to do exploratory operations to try to find a pinched nerve that did not show on any of the tests, but in most of these exploratory surgeries, nothing is found. In a typical case, the patient confronted with the fact that nothing was found may ask quite pointedly, "Where is this pain coming from, doctor?" And before the doctor can answer, he adds, "Certainly this pain isn't in my head, we both know that!" The pain is so real and the patient seems so adequate that it is hard for anyone to believe that this could be psychosomatic pain. But it is. I have seen as many as four exploratory back surgeries done on a patient until both doctor and patient gave up, but by that time, there was considerable real pain and disability as a result of the surgeries. Finally the patient's "choice" was confirmed. The same can go for duodenal ulcer, ileitis, colitis, and most pain associated with the digestive tract.

This doesn't mean that you shouldn't go to the doctor and get a good examination to find out if you have appendicitis or some other real sickness, but if the examination is essentially negative, that bit of "good news" not only does not relieve the pain but sometimes makes it worse. Confronted with your own inadequacy, and having already decided you can't handle it, you choose to continue to hurt. Partly you are desperately trying to prove to the doctor that it is not you who is at fault but he, and partly you are trying to prove the same thing to yourself. It is not the purpose of this book to deal specifically with psychosomatic diseases but they are plentiful. For example, arthritis to some degree is psychosomatic, as are high blood pressure, sinus trouble, asthma, perhaps even coronary artery disease, since the coronary type is a high striver who isn't succeeding up to his own aspirations. This does not deny that the physical component of these diseases should be treated even if the psychological is not. We must understand that many people are willing to pay a huge price in sickness and disability to avoid facing the reality of their inability to find happiness. Sometimes even drastic treatment for psychosomatic disease is frustrating, as in surgery to remove the lower half of the stomach, the acid-secreting half, which when some people are upset oversecretes acid and undersecretes the normal protective substance. Then the acid attacks the duodenum to produce an ulcer. Surgery almost always clears the ulcer, a fact that you would think would make a patient ecstatically happy, but in many cases he becomes seriously depressed. There are articles in the literature describing suicide because the depression is so severe. Painful as it was, the ulcer was his friend. Although the "friend" may have endangered his life, it did reduce the pain.

Sometimes, however, almost the converse of this occurs when a very serious disease can make a symptom choice unnecessary, or perhaps supersede it if the disease threatens the very basic need to stay alive. While I made the argument earlier that for most of us there is more to life than staying alive, in the long run, a short, acute, real, externally caused disease can sometimes temporarily "cure" a person deeply involved in choosing one of the symptom categories. For example, when I was a psychiatric resident I was in charge of fifty-four patients on the ward of the VA mental hospital in Los Angeles. I would make my rounds every day trying to get involved, trying to help, trying to show that I cared. One patient was especially difficult and I dreaded going up to him. Rather than shake my hand, he would sometimes spit at me, usually at the floor in front of me, while he cursed me and said if I was any good as a doctor I would help him get rid of the monkey that lived on his back and tortured him. It was very difficult for a young doctor, imbued with psychiatric fervor, to face the inadequacy of this fervor in dealing with this man's total immersion in his choice to be crazy. One day, after perhaps seven or eight weeks, when I came to him on regular morning rounds he said very quietly and rationally, "Doctor, I would like to see you after rounds in your office." I was startled but said, "Yes, of course." When I finished he very quietly accompanied me to my office. You might think that I would be afraid to go into the office with someone ordinarily threatening and hostile, but he was obviously rational—had chosen to be so—at the time and it never occurred to me to be afraid. I took him into the office. He said, "Doctor, I think I am sick." I asked what was wrong and he said, "I have a severe pain in my chest and I'm having trouble breathing. Would you examine me?" When I examined his chest, it was obvious that he was filled with fluid. He also had a high fever. He was suffering from a very severe case of lobar pneumonia. If he hadn't gotten good medical care he would have died. I walked him to the medical ward and introduced him to the doctors there who would take care of him. He was very cordial. He had suddenly, with his pneumonia, become a completely cooperative patient. All the time he was in the medical ward he showed no signs of psychosis, the need to stay alive temporarily superseding his need for love and worth. Now, don't misconstrue this and believe that the cure of psychosis is to threaten people with life itself, a course which, incidentally, has often been tried and works poorly. But if it happens spontaneously from within the person and if it is short term, it may be temporarily effective. After about three weeks he recovered from his pneumonia and went back to the ward, where he gradually returned to his previous crazy behavior. He never again treated me badly—he now shook my hand and thanked me —but he returned the monkey to his back and his psychosis was much the same as before except that he did accept me as a human being because I had helped him get over his pneumonia. Interestingly enough, it was difficult for the people in the medical ward to understand why in the world this man was in the mental hospital because he seemed so rational and cooperative. I had to take some of them onto the ward two or three months later to prove that he was not unjustly incarcerated.

This, then, describes the four symptom categories, one or more of which many people choose to reduce the pain of failure. In most cases the symptom eventually allows the person to ask for help for a problem that seems to others to have happened to him, rather than something he has chosen. People continually look for reinforcement from others to confirm that they are not at fault, that they did not choose their symptoms, they happened to them. The girls at the school for delinquents where I worked used to tell me their problem was not that they were thieves or runaways, but that they were emotionally disturbed. (In the comic song "Officer Krupke" from *West Side Story*, this point is beautifully illustrated.) This does not mean that people who make the symptom choices can't be helped through good psychiatric treatment to find love and worth, but it does mean that we should not be confused by the symptom either into believing the person is so "sick" he can't get this help, or into feeling so sorry for him that we do not work with him to help himself. No one is so inadequate that he can't help himself to some degree. Not only can he, but he must; nothing else will work. In my book *Reality Therapy* I describe how to do this in some detail, but the point here is to explain how weak people choose to suffer and how they may help *themselves* to become stronger. To do this I will advocate gaining strength through a positive addiction. But before we can understand positive addiction, the common but not well understood problem of negative addiction must be explained.

NEGATIVE ADDICTION—
THE THIRD CHOICE OF THE WEAK

Addiction, that is, negative addiction, is the third, and in terms of pain, essentially successful choice in the series of choices made by people who are unable to find sufficient love and worth. Each choice—from the initial decision to give up trying to find love or worth, the second choice to take on one or more symptoms, and the final choice of becoming addicted—is a pain-reducing step. The reason addiction is powerful and difficult to break is that it alone of all the choices consistently both completely relieves the pain of failure, and provides an intensely pleasurable experience. It could be argued that the intense pleasure came from relieving the pain of failure. For example, a man who has been on the desert without water for three days is in ecstasy when he is given a cool drink. While I am sure that an addict always has that experience I believe he has much more. The addiction, whichever one he chooses, provides him with an intense pleasure over and above the satisfaction of finally getting rid of the pain. It is this peculiar, unique combination of pain relief first and then, quickly, a "rush" of pleasure that is necessary for an addiction.

The pain relief is very specific—it is relief from the pain of the failure to find love and worth. Addicting drugs also have the ability to relieve any overwhelming psychological pain, even the fear of dying. Morphine, for example, is lifesaving to relax the patient who has just suffered a heart attack but unless he has other serious deficiencies in his life the heart-attack victim will not become a morphine addict. Once he is out of danger he will no longer feel a powerful need for the drug. Therefore, to become addicted the person must have a large amount of pain associated with one or more of the symptoms. If this is present, and it is in millions of people, then two drugs seem most able to provide the unique combination of both relief and pleasure—alcohol and heroin. Both of these drugs have close relatives which are also addicting but from long experience they are preferred to their less effective kin.

Typically a negative addict is a person who is severely frustrated in his own particular search for love and worth. He made the first choice to give up usually when he was very young. As a second choice he may have tried acting out for a while but for him it was not very successful and he usually switched to depression or to a psychosomatic symptom. Then he is introduced to alcohol or heroin and suddenly, miraculously, not only is the pain gone but it is replaced by an intense pleasure that he has never before experienced. It is as if you were a star football player and in the third quarter you injured your ankle. It is excruciatingly painful but the coach desperately needs you as it's the final championship game. At that time both you and the coach want to win the game so badly your future health is unimportant. The team doctor shoots novocaine into your ankle and the pain disappears. You win the game, the championship, and you bask in glory, but in the process you have torn your ankle to shreds and limp for the rest of your life. When the glory wears off the pain returns forever. Similarly, an addict tears his life to shreds; his addiction, which provides him with "glory" where in the past he had only pain, overpowers every other urge within him and he devotes his life to the addicting drug or behavior. To that end he is willing to give up principles, ideals, family, friends, or spouse; nothing in his life is allowed to stand against the drug or other addiction. He lives by one set of values, which is that whatever promotes his addiction is right, everything else is wrong. If the drug is illegal, as is heroin, he will lie, cheat, steal, and on rare occasions kill to get both the relief and the pleasure the drug provides. Even if the drug is legal, as is alcohol, the alcoholic will let little or nothing stand between him and his bottle. The major difference between heroin and alcohol is that, contrary to popular belief, heroin has no physically harmful effect. Alcohol is physically harmful to the brain, to the liver, to the nerve endings, eventually perhaps even to the stomach and intestines. Both drugs seem equally addicting, and why a person chooses one over another is probably based on experience, on availability, on legality, and on some personal idiosyncrasy not yet understood. What we do know is that the drugs work to relieve the pain and provide pleasure to those people who have made a second choice and are looking for a third.

While it may be an overstatement to say that all addicting drugs ruin a person's life, it probably is safe to say that under our present system anyone who gets addicted to heroin, which is both illegal and very expensive, stands a good chance of having his life ruined. There is little indication that anyone who is addicted to alcohol can lead a productive life either. While these are the major addicting drugs there are also many food addicts in this country with its abundance. They overeat until they become obese, sometimes grotesquely so. Stuffing themselves relieves their pain and provides pleasure. I once had a young woman as a patient who told me that when she is lonely and depressed because she believes her husband doesn't love her, she goes into the kitchen, takes a loaf of white bread wrapped in waxed paper, opens up the end, and systematically removes one piece after another and stuffs it into her mouth and swallows it until the loaf is finished. This obviously is an addiction. Possibly, if we could break all the food addicts and incipient food addicts from their addictions, we would have enough food to feed millions of the world's starving people. They eat an unbelievable amount.

There is at least one addicting behavior, gambling—an addiction that causes the addict to gamble away all of his money and all the money he can beg, borrow, or steal. I don't want to argue whether gambling addicts want to lose—I doubt it—but it is the pleasure of the game that drives them, win or lose. They usually lose because they never quit, and the odds against them prevail in the long run. Under gambling I also include workaholics, who are addicted to exciting, wheeling-and-dealing jobs. These people often win at work—some are big winners but they remain addicted as long as they win. Losing may break their habit. This theory goes against the idea that gamblers want to lose, and there are probably more gamblers in the world of business than at the tables of Las Vegas. To bear out my point that it's the brinkmanship of gambling that attracts the workaholic, I don't think that even if we look hard, we will find many people addicted to picking up garbage or typing in an insurance company.

Finally, there are two minor addicting drugs, nicotine and caffeine, which are not particularly dangerous to a person's health or lifestyle and which do not do much to relieve the intense pain of someone with severe symptoms. They do, however, singly and often very well in combination, pleasurably relieve the tensions of everyday living for the strong as well as the weak, so much so that for almost all who use them they are next to impossible to give up. Some people claim that nicotine is the most addicting of all drugs, if addicting means hard to kick, but no negative addict would trade alcohol or heroin for cigarettes and coffee. So regardless of the danger (coffee seems safe enough), few people will trade the present pleasure that nicotine gives for better health twenty-five or thirty years in the future. Many of those who kick the nicotine habit report that even after many years have gone by the desire for the nicotine never leaves.

It should be mentioned, however, that many besides addicts enjoy alcohol, gambling, and large amounts of food. If they run into periods of failure there is always the danger of addiction, but most people are strong enough so there is little risk this will happen to them. More than 90 percent of the people who drink have no serious problem with alcohol but that remaining 10 percent is a huge number. Some estimate there are 10 million alcoholics in the USA alone. Heroin also may be used in moderation by many people, but because it is illegal there is little data on those who "chip" for pleasure but are not addicted. We know, however, that there were many soldiers in Vietnam in the sixties and seventies who used an extremely pure form of heroin, and it was feared that when they came home we would have a wave of new addicts. That this hasn't occurred shows that they were able to use heroin for pleasure or relief, probably both, in an extremely stressful, painful situation where reality was overwhelming. Once home where they could resume a normal life they had no overpowering desire to continue the use of this illegal drug. Maybe if it were legal they would still use it, but even with fairly extensive use only a few became addicts.[*] Perhaps some of them have become alcoholics,[†] since it is known that heroin users when they do give up heroin usually

[*]D. H. Davis, D. W. Goodwin, and L. N. Robbins, "Drinking Amid Abundant Illicit Drugs," Archives of General Psychiatry, Vol. 32, No. 2 (February 1975), p. 230.
[†]Ibid.

become alcoholics.* But I suspect the number is not high or there would be some report on it.

The obvious problem of addiction is that the addict, through his addiction, is able to live with little love or worth, without having to suffer the pain of failing to get it. In fact, he enjoys his life if his addiction is satisfied, and has no need for anything else. His credo is why search for something as tenuous, in his experience, as love and worth when his addiction is sure. It goes without saying that the pleasure of addiction depends on a regular supply (love and worth do too) of whatever you are addicted to. If deprived of your addiction you must return not only to the pain and misery of your previous second-choice symptoms but to the additional pain, mental and physical, that comes with withdrawal. In alcohol and heroin and food the addiction is both physical and mental, in gambling it's all mental, but for practical purposes they all hurt when they are stopped. You miss what you have got used to having and you suffer.

It is this pain coupled with the pleasure of the drug that locks an addict into his habit. To quit means to return to both the painful symptom plus the added pain of withdrawal, which means that very suddenly the addict has to have a lot of love and worth to make up for all that suffering. Since on his own he couldn't get them before he became addicted, his chances now are nil. That means that merely depriving an addict of his addiction will neither weaken his habit nor break it. Alcoholics and heroin addicts are in jail for years without losing their desire for their drug. Their only chance to kick their habit is through organizations like AA or Daytop Village. Like all successful anti-addiction organizations these strive to give the addict an opportunity for much more love and worth

*Edward Brecher, "Licit and Illicit Drugs," *Consumers Union Report* (1972), p. 85

than he ordinarily has any chance to get by himself, so that with this excess infusion he sometimes is able to make the choice of trying to exist without his drug. The more love and worth he is able to get through the organization the more successful he will be in his recovery. Even though I feel AA wrongly labels alcoholism as a disease, it still provides good treatment and is, I believe, the single most successful anti-addiction organization we have. In its program of intensive human and spiritual support, love, care, and concern, the alcoholic gets relief from his pain and begins to restructure his life so that he can get pleasure without alcohol. Although he rarely loses the desire to drink, he gains enough strength through his newfound love and worth to make not drinking a possible choice. The fact is, however, that he has to remain a member of the organization for life. It is the rare addict who is able to gain the strength to continue to abstain without the support of the group. For hard drugs like heroin the most successful organizations are live-in—the addict may have to live for years, maybe for life, in Synanon or Daytop Village, or he won't be strong enough to stay clean. That doesn't mean the programs are inadequate; it means the problem is tough.

It may seem incongruous to say that an addict is weak. No one seems more hard-working or persistent. Once addicted and driven by the pleasure of his addiction, he is extremely strong. Perhaps our most self-sufficient citizens are heroin addicts hustling each day for their habit. They are the ultimate in the work ethic, struggling by themselves against overwhelming odds to fulfill their need. But this strength is all tied to addiction; when it comes to finding love and worth they seem to have no strength at all. Evidently the pleasure of their habit is far stronger than any pleasure they can remember or imagine could come from love and worth. Just as those people who have love and worth find it intensely pleasurable and not only don't become addicts (if they use addicting drugs it is in extreme moderation), they can't even *imagine* becoming addicts. It seems logical to conclude that if an addict put all the effort he puts into his addiction into finding love and worth he certainly would be successful, *but very specifically that is what he can't do.* He doesn't have that kind of strength. What he has, and I think this is the best way to describe it, is short-term strength. He has the strength over any short haul to find his addicting drug (the drug itself may provide some of this strength, as we will see later), but to find love and worth is a long-term chancy search, a strength he neither has nor wants. Why take the long road if the short one is better? He never does unless his hand is forced.

Finally and most important, to find happiness *we need others,* but an addict *needs only himself.* Dependent only upon himself and knowing he can pursue his addiction, he does so with a single-minded devotion that is remarkable to behold. But what if there were addictions that, instead of making you weaker, *made you stronger?* Since the title of this book is *Positive Addiction* it is obvious that I believe they exist. Therefore, now that the importance of strength has been established, it is time to take a look at the positive side of addiction.

two

POSITIVE ADDICTION—HOW ANYONE, WEAK OR STRONG, CAN GAIN STRENGTH

In the summer of 1973, while on vacation, I read a book by Roger Kahn called *The Boys of Summer.* This book described the Brooklyn Dodgers championship team of 1953, the team with Roy Campanella, Jackie Robinson, Peewee Reese, Gil Hodges, Duke Snider, and others. It tells about them as they were in 1952, when Roger Kahn covered them as a cub reporter for the New York *Post,* and some of them as they were twenty years later. One of the players he visited was George "Shotgun" Shuba, and in recalling the old days with him at his home in Youngstown, Kahn said, "George, one thing you always had was a great natural swing." Schuba laughed and said, "Let me tell you a little more about my natural swing." He then described how as a sixteen-year-old he had made up his mind to be a major-league ballplayer. He didn't want to go into the steel mills in Youngstown where his family traditionally worked. He knew he had good baseball skills and he was smart enough to know that even though he had made up his mind to try to reach the majors there was a long way to go. He decided he could probably learn to field well enough but he knew he would have to learn to hit major-league pitching, which many experts say is the most difficult of all athletic skills. He had noticed that all good hitters have a great swing and decided that one thing he could do on his own was to improve his. He knotted a piece of string so that a row of knots covered the strike zone from top to bottom, and hung it from a rafter in his basement. He then took a heavily weighted bat and every day from age sixteen through his minor-league career and into the majors—that is, every day he didn't play major-league ball—he swung the weighted bat at the strike zone on the piece of string *six hundred times.*

When I read that anecdote and visualized Shuba swinging that bat six hundred times a day in his basement something went ping in my mind. I am not myself physically disciplined and the idea of a sixteen-year-old kid swinging a weighted bat each day six hundred times a day on faith, with no guarantees at all except that he would tire himself out, struck me as almost superhuman. I know the world is full of stories about people who have incredible self-discipline. I am sure there are great pianists who played the piano sixteen hours a day and great runners who ran twenty miles a day for years, but what they did was more directly applicable to where they were going. I could have seen Shuba more clearly in my mind out hitting batting practice each day for a couple of hours if he could have arranged to have a ball thrown to him, but religiously doing something as chancy as swinging a bat by himself in his basement year after year—this really got to me. I said to myself, how did he do it? How did he keep it up? (A friend of mine has interviewed Shuba and confirmed the fact that he did do it, and that he did keep it up.) What then ran through my mind (and George Shuba really doesn't like this label because he thinks it is pejorative) was the only way he could have done it was far beyond what we usually call willpower. If all he had was willpower I don't believe he could have gone so long; there had to be something else; and right then, although I hadn't any idea how, I came to the conclusion that what had happened was that he became addicted to swinging the bat. The idea of being hooked on bat swinging seemed silly and when I shared the idea with my family we all laughed but I still couldn't get it out of my head. It doesn't seem silly now, because after thinking about this idea almost obsessively for the next eighteen months, I believe that is exactly what happened. He swung the bat for a period of time, probably three or four months, on pure willpower, then slowly, and with no awareness, he became addicted to this exercise. If he missed swinging the bat he felt some kind of pain or misery or upset, perhaps some anxiety or guilt, some discomfort, which was sufficient to push him to do it each day. The classic signs of addiction were there. When he stopped he suffered and the suffering was relieved only by the addicting activity. He confirms that he was uncomfortable if he didn't do it. Shuba seems to be not only a very truthful person but a strong, mildly stoic character, so if he says he was uncomfortable, I think that would mean more discomfort than his statement indicates. What I believe is that Shuba had a mild positive addiction to an activity that he believed would help him and which I believe not only helped him physically to become a better hitter, but also helped him mentally to gain the strength to fight his way to the major leagues.

When I was mulling this over back in July 1973, I was still a long way from the concept of positive addiction, as I will describe it in this chapter. My first observation, which still holds true, is that a positive addiction increases your mental strength and is the opposite of a negative addiction, which seems to sap the strength from every part of your life except in the area of the addiction. For example, an alcoholic is strong in his quest for alcohol but weak in his desire for anything else. Negative addicts are totally involved with their addiction, having long since given up on finding love and worth. The positive addict enjoys his addiction but it does not dominate his life. From it he gains *mental* strength which he uses to help himself accomplish whatever he tries to do more successfully. Unlike a negative addict, who is satisfied completely to live for his addiction, to the exclusion of everything else, a positive addict uses his extra strength to gain more love and more worth, more pleasure, more meaning, more zest from life in general. Positive addiction is especially valuable because it is a way in which anyone by himself can increase his strength. Every other way in which we gain strength depends on others, either for more love or more recognition, but no matter how lonely or how worthless you may be, if you can become positively addicted you can gain strength. You can then use this strength to gain more love and more worth. Since most people who are weak lack love and friendship, they are cut off from the main way to help themselves; they are locked into a vicious cycle of weakness. If we could learn through positive addiction to break this cycle, as I am sure millions have, then anyone strong or weak, with no more friends or recognition than he or she now has, could become stronger.

As I thought about Shuba reaching the majors partly through swinging that weighted bat, almost immediately I began to think of two sons of a good friend of mine, young men who in the early sixties, when they were beginning college, were going through the usual existential anxieties of that time. Their preoccupation with "What is this all about?" "Where will it get me?" "Is it really worthwhile to do this, that, or something else?" caused their concerned father to ask me if I had any suggestions. I knew him well, knew that he and his wife had been excellent parents, and I knew his sons. We didn't talk much, I just said, "You have a right to be concerned but I think somehow or other everything will work out okay." That may sound like poor advice for an anxious parent, but if the parents are effective people the advice is usually sound. A couple of months later my friend told me that both his sons had become involved with transcendental meditation, taught by the Maharishi Mahesh Yogi, that they were meditating quite faithfully, that they seemed enthusiastic about the process, and most important, it seemed to help them to settle down in college. At that time I didn't believe in the intrinsic value of meditation. I had the usual skepticism of the ignorant, but I said any self-imposed discipline was good and certainly there seemed to be no way it could hurt them. I thought that meditation was a fad and would soon wear off but neither son accepted it as a fad and it didn't wear off. They continued; both of them still meditate regularly and both of them have done remarkably well in their personal lives. They are strong and believe they have gained a sizable portion of this strength through the process of meditation, and now I think they have too. Today I believe that meditation, transcendental or otherwise, is a form, albeit a mental form rather than a physical form, of positive addiction. When I recently talked over the concept of positive addiction with one of my friend's sons he confirmed, both for himself and for other meditators he knows well, that there is an annoying discomfort, a guilty, queasy feeling they and many meditators experience if they skip their meditation period any day. They meditate faithfully twenty to thirty minutes twice a day, usually about the same time morning and afternoon, carefully following the instructions of their teacher, the Maharishi. Some days they meditate a little more but they don't meditate all day long, any more than Shuba swung the bat all day long, so initially it seemed apparent to me that whatever a positive addiction is, it is not something that you do all day long. It is not like searching for heroin or drinking alcohol or gambling, which may occupy you practically all the time. It is something you do for a reasonable time, usually about an hour a day.

That much seemed clear but I still had a lot to learn because I don't meditate and I certainly don't swing a bat. The reason I don't, or at least the reason I tell myself I don't, is that these activities seem to be such a drag, so patently boring that I can't conceive of having the discipline even to get started, much less continue. Therefore, my first impression of positive addiction was that it had to be an unpleasant experience, it had to be an activity during which you were conquering pain or enduring boredom. The old puritan ethic that few of us have completely kicked prevailed in my initial impression that anything that could do you good had to be a little miserable, the old eat-your-spinach type of thinking that still exists in many of our minds.

But the meditators claim that meditation is not unpleasant; it is pleasant almost from the beginning, sometimes from the very first time. They say as one gets deeply into it and becomes a more accomplished meditator, the enjoyment increases. They insist that there is never anything unpleasant about it if it is done correctly. Playing the devil's advocate I have asked many meditators why they don't meditate all day if it is so pleasant, but they say, "No, that's not the point; it is not something you would want to do all day." You meditate to use its benefits in the rest of your life; it would be pointless to do it all day long—twenty minutes twice a day is sufficient. If you think about it, the time it took to swing a bat the way Shuba swung it is probably about five to six seconds; if he swung it six hundred times that would be thirty to thirty-six thousand seconds or about fifty to sixty minutes a day. More and more, as I study positive addiction in its various forms, it seems that about an hour a day does it. Therefore, if the person who is looking to be positively addicted isn't willing to put in this forty minutes to an hour a day there is a good chance that whatever he chooses to try to become addicted to won't be successful. Some people, of course, spend more time with their positive addictions but very few people are able to develop a positive addiction by spending less than forty minutes to an hour a day, in one or two sessions, but usually in not more than two.

At this point I was willing to accept the hour a day but I was still unable to accept the fact that meditation or any other form of positive addiction was pleasant. I knew that the meditators I was in contact with were almost all proselytizing and, like most of those who push their thing, they were gilding the lily, they were not willing to tell me the truth about its boredom. Still on that boredom-endurance kick, the following winter I began to ask for reactions about positive addiction from the audiences to whom I frequently speak.

After a regular talk I would give a short description of positive addiction (PA) and then ask people who thought they were positively addicted to meet with me afterward and tell me about their experiences. In Irvine, California, an attractive man of about thirty, beautifully dressed in monk's robes, came up to me and said, "I think I have a positive addiction. I chant the psalms every day for an hour." I continued to look at him, still not understanding exactly what he meant, and he told me, "I used to be an alcoholic, a down-in-the-bottom-of-the-barrel alcoholic, and then seeing my life going down the drain I decided I had to do something. My drinking was completely ruining my life." Somehow, and he really couldn't explain how he decided to do it, he began to chant the psalms. We talked about the Gregorian monks who chant routinely, but he didn't think that was exactly why. He didn't really know. All he knew was he began to chant for an hour a day. And as he chanted, he said, "I began to pull myself together. I began to get strength, I stopped drinking.

I attracted a few followers and I was able to start a little monastery." As he was attractively dressed in his robes, obviously his little monastery has prospered. He said, "We do good work. I am leading what I think is a fulfilled life and I no longer drink at all." I said, "Do you still chant the psalms?" and he replied, "Every day for an hour." I said, "Do you enjoy it?" and he laughed and said, "I hate it." It was this statement, "I hate it," coupled with my still strong belief that a positive addiction must be to some degree uncomfortable that made me think for some time, even after the meditators denied it, that positive addicts really don't like their actual addiction, which does them good, in contrast to negative addicts, who like what they do even though it harms them. I hated to give this idea up because it seemed to wrap things up so neatly —negative addiction feels good but does harm, positive addiction feels lousy but does good. The alcoholic-turned-monk reinforced this neat conclusion when I asked him, "If you hate it, why do you keep doing it?" He said, "I am hooked— if I don't chant I suffer worse than doing it." He described his withdrawal pains as almost the same kind of discomfort he had when, on occasion, he had tried to stop drinking. Because it seemed so logical I wanted to believe it, and I didn't question him further. If I could question him more now I believe I would find that while he doesn't exactly get a buzz out of the actual process of chanting the psalms, as I doubt Schuba enjoyed swinging the bat that much, something goes on in his brain that is so pleasurable that it more than counteracts the fairly deadly boring addictive process he has chosen. I believe that what goes on within positive addicts' minds feels extremely good, and this particular pleasure, which when they experience it becomes extremely important to them, can't be obtained easily or as well in any other way. While the activity itself may be grueling or boring, it causes a pleasurable mental effect while it goes on, and often after, that makes the whole experience so pleasing that it is addicting.

It was at this point that I developed a short questionnaire and began to pass it out at places where the audience granted me the extra time to discuss PA. First, I would describe what I then knew about PA and then ask those in the audience who believed they might be positively addicted to fill out the questionnaire. Many people responded, many more than I believed would. Not all are what I would now term positive addicts but quite a few undoubtedly are. Among the people who responded was a large number of runners, of whom I was at best dimly aware. But as more and more responded I found out that North America is filled with runners, people who run every day for at least an hour, some of whom run competitively, but most don't. *And these runners are almost all addicted to running.* I had never thought much about runners. I knew they existed because I would see them out in the morning on days when I left to catch an early plane. They were mostly running on San Vicente, a boulevard in my neighborhood that seems to attract them. Most of them looked as if they were in pain and many of them, I learned later, never miss a day. What in the world makes these people run? I suppose they get started with the idea that they will build themselves up, keep trim or healthy, maybe prevent a heart attack, but I don't believe this many people are capable of that kind of voluntary, painful, lonely, boring self-improvement if that is all they get out of it. I am not saying being in good shape isn't worth a lot, but I believe they have to get something more. I don't think it is possible to do something that seems to be such a painful drag in order to get some indefinite future payoff like not having a heart attack twenty years later. Even the present payoff of being trim and strong doesn't seem that motivating to me and I don't think it is. I keep pretty trim playing tennis, which is

45

more fun than running your guts out before breakfast. Or at least that's the way it seemed to me. The clue to what drives runners to run came from a man in Toronto who, when I was discussing positive addiction, raised his hand and said, "I would like to tell you about my addiction." He looked to be about sixty years old, he was trim, he spoke well. He said, "I am addicted to running." He said he has been at it for almost seven years, he runs every day and missed only two days all last year when the snow was so high he couldn't get out of the house. Those days he ran in place in the house but it wasn't quite the same. I asked, "What happens if you don't run?" and he said, "I am so miserable that really I have no choice. I have to go out and run because I don't want the misery." He said, "If I can't run in the morning I run later that afternoon or evening," but he prefers to start his day with a run. This is common to runners; most of them like to start the day with a run. He runs by himself and has no desire to run with anyone else. He says when another runner tries to join him he prefers to turn off, a significant statement I'll shortly explain. He seemed to be verifying most of my ideas, as they were then, but when, with a laugh, he added something else, I got what I believe is a fundamental insight into the true nature of all positive addiction—the *PA state of mind.* This occurred when he said there was only one problem with his running—it was dangerous. Everyone in the room looked at him when he said that and many of us laughed. When I asked, "What could be dangerous about running in Toronto the first thing in the morning by yourself for an hour?" he went on to explain that almost every day when he runs, he quickly goes into some kind of a trancelike mental state. His description is, "I just let my mind go and when I'm really *into a run* [a common term for running addicts to use] I am not completely aware of my surroundings. I will run across streets, I run through red lights, I have narrowly missed being hit by cars

46

on several occasions." He described how careful he must be when he runs because he almost always gets into this mental state. As we talked more about this experience he said it seemed to be a process of letting your mind go, letting your mind spin free. He said, "Your mind is there but it is not there —it's in sort of a transcendental, trancelike state." Since that time I have talked to many more physically addicted people, runners and others, and it is this state of mind that almost all of them describe, a trancelike, transcendental mental state that accompanies the addictive exercise. *I believe now that it is this same state, the positive addiction (PA) state of mind, that the exercisers reach indirectly and that the meditators are trying to reach directly. That is the core of positive addiction* (and also the core of negative addiction as I will explain later, in Chapter Three). I think the monk often reached this state when he chanted the psalms and Schuba reached it frequently through swinging the bat. Whatever it is, and no matter how it is reached, almost everyone describes it as extremely pleasurable, very relaxing; and although they find it difficult to put what they experience into words, all of them agree that they reach it, whatever it is, and that it feels very, very good. They also say that for them it cannot be reached easily in any other way except through their addictive activity.

In March 1973, *Psychology Today* published an article* about exercise. At Purdue University the authors asked a large, random group of generally sedentary middle-aged people to enter a three-month planned and directed daily exercise program to see if they could build themselves up physically. To check them, they did not only pre- and post-physical tests but also some before and after psychological evalua-

*A. H. Ismail and L. E. Trachtman, "Jogging the Imagination," *Psychology Today*, Vol. 6, No. 10 (March 1973), pp. 78–82.

tions. I was so intrigued by the results that I wrote to Professor Ismail, who ran the program. He reported that none of the people who entered the program became addicted to any of the exercises, that is, no one who entered the program is still doing at least one exercise for an hour a day. About four of the participants have continued after the program disbanded but only for about thirty minutes no more than three times a week. Nevertheless, even without addiction, the exercise program, which included a lot of running, caused these people, when they were psychologically tested, to show three significant changes after three months of exercise, two of which puzzled the authors of the article. They showed an increase in self-confidence, an increase in their power of imagination, and also an increase in nonspecific guilt—that is, they felt guilty about something but about what they were not clear. The authors felt, because they did build themselves up physically, the increase in confidence was predictable. The increase in imagination came as a mild surprise, but the guilt they couldn't explain at all. It seems to me that if they had more confidence then they had more mental strength, and an increase in imagination could be expected as part of that increased mental strength. Certainly an active imagination is part of the fuller and richer lives that most strong, confident people lead. This much is not too difficult to explain, but if the authors had been aware of PA they also would have been able to predict the increase in guilt. What happened was that while none of the exercisers became addicted, many of them experienced, during the exercise, the PA state of mind. They began to feel their minds spinning free, briefly and probably haphazardly, as part of a good day's workout. They didn't get much of this because, as I will explain more in detail later, the program wasn't set up to promote positive addiction. It was a group program, it was directed, and they were to some degree coerced into it. Still, their minds did spin free for short periods, enough to get them to experience brief periods of the PA state, and when they quit they felt guilty because they sensed, without knowing, that they were leaving something of potentially great pleasure and great value to them. Since it was a three-month program, when it ended, like most people, they quit. A few continued, as I said, on an individual, voluntary basis, but not to the extent that I would call them positive addicts. I am sure their main motivation was to try to keep the physical benefits they may have got, but that they never really experienced more than a fleeting taste of the potential mental benefits. This taste of PA, however, was enough to account for the increase in guilt the tests showed. Had they decided to exercise on their own they might have become positive addicts, but they exercised as part of a program and they let the program set the boundaries. When it was over they quit. This is much different from Schuba, the monk, the meditators, or the runner in Toronto, all of whom decided to do their thing on their own. It seems to me, therefore, that to reach PA takes some personal initiative and you are much less likely to reach it if you enter a program than if you decide to do whatever it is that might get you addicted on your own. If the Maharishi had classes where people meditated together, I believe it wouldn't work nearly as well. He teaches them the process but then it is up to them to transcend on their own. He has some trappings of Eastern mysticism, like offering flowers and fruit, but regardless of whether these are important or not (and I don't believe they are), he makes sure to instruct his students to meditate on their own. Therefore, I believe another factor can be added to PA: whatever the state of positive addiction is, it is almost always easier to reach it if you decide to do whatever you do on your own. It is not a group activity. Even when people do the activity in groups, like running together, they must keep to themselves or they won't reach the desired state. This doesn't mean that a group run is not an enjoyable social event, but on these days few will reach the PA state. The PA state is a state of oneness, not a group experience, and why this is will be explained shortly.

A further finding seems to be that to reach PA takes time, probably longer than it takes for a person to develop a negative addiction. It is possible, however, that it only seems this way. If you count all the years of failure, suffering, and symptoms that precede a negative addiction, reaching PA may be quicker. It rarely occurs in less than six months no matter what the activity, and some runners and meditators say it took them two years. Here it must be stated that not all those who attempt any potential PA activity like meditation or running will reach PA. One has to keep going a long time on faith and most people don't have that much faith. It is interesting, and I will explain this in more detail later in the book, that most PA activities are quickly beneficial whether or not the practitioner reaches the PA state of mind regularly. For that reason many of those who meditate are able to keep going because meditation, unlike running, does not take much effort. To get the peak benefit, however, one has to become addicted and only a small percentage, around 10 percent of the meditators, are able to reach PA. Since there are so many of them, however, they still make up the single largest group of positive addicts.

The other large group on whom I have some data are the runners, and for them it also takes at least six months and most of them seem to have to run vigorously for almost a year before they reach PA. This means they have to endure the pain of running on the faith that it is doing them some good physically, because until they run long enough to reach the PA state regularly they can have no clear idea of what this unique mental experience is. Other runners may tell them of it, but hearing about it and experiencing it are two different things, and generally runners don't talk much about this part of their running experience. They don't because, partly, they don't clearly recognize what it is and also because it is hard to describe. Many do recognize it but still don't talk about it because they believe that someone who hasn't experienced the PA state will think they are a little screwy. To nonrunners, running as a head trip makes little sense. Besides, it takes so long to reach PA through running that I doubt if the far-off mental benefits have motivated many runners. They start running to get in shape, and if they get the plus of becoming addicted it usually happens so slowly that, as I just said, many are barely aware of what has happened to them. All they know is that it feels good and that it hurts if they stop. Therefore, it takes self-discipline or a great deal of strength to start (much more than it takes to meditate), but if you run for a year, if you run mostly alone, if you get up to at least an hour a day in which you do at least six to eight miles or more, you will very likely become positively addicted to running. Once that happens you will probably keep running as long as you can. Runners in their eighties are not uncommon.

But whether it is running, which is hard, and almost always addicting to those who persist, or meditating, which is less hard physically and not nearly so addicting, it is significant that positive addiction, like all good things in life, is most open to people who have the strength to stick to it. It takes strength to make the commitment to yourself—and it really must be to yourself and not to someone else—to do your addictive thing for a sufficient period of time to reach PA. While it seems that it takes less strength to reach PA through meditating than through running, this may not be true. It is possible that meditation takes a different kind of strength and is no more available to someone who is weak than physical exercise. It also may be possible that the PA state cannot be reached by everyone in the same way. It may be that some people can reach it only through meditating, others through running, others through some other way. Later, when I discuss the relationship of self-criticism to positive addiction, there may be some indication of why some reach it more easily physically than mentally. Nevertheless, I suspect that running does take more strength and I would suggest that a person who has a track record of giving up easily go into meditation rather than running, swimming, bike riding, or the more strenuous physical activities if he wishes to reach PA.

To summarize, at this point in my thinking I was able to say that a positive addiction is something that people choose to do, physical or mental. They believe it has some value for them, and it is something that they can do on their own. It is something they believe has enough worth to put about an hour a day into doing, perhaps in one period, usually in no more than two. It is something that they think they can become proficient in doing because if they can't see that they are attaining some proficiency they will rarely continue long enough to reach PA. It has to have an inherent value in itself so that they will stick to it long enough to reach the PA state, which, in many cases, may take up to a year. Once they have reached PA it is easily recognized by the fact that if they attempt to stop the activity they suffer withdrawal, some sort of pain, discomfort, anxiety, or guilt that is satisfactorily relieved only by resuming the activity. Like negative addicts, they will continue if they are able because, unlike a negative addiction, there is no reason to try to kick PA—not only does it feel extremely good, but it also gives strength.

Now that I have established the basic criteria for positive addiction more needs to be explained. For example, what makes this condition occur? What happens after several months of running or meditating which allows us literally to let our brains alone, to let them spin free? I believe there must be one unifying factor that makes PA possible whether we meditate, run, do yoga, or swim. About a year after I became aware of the concept of positive addiction I stumbled upon this factor, which, I believe, is not only the key to positive addiction, but has major implications of helping in the rest of our lives. Let me explain how this happened and then try to give some evidence for what I claim.

As I was searching for this factor, a friend of mine who knows I am a tennis player sent me a book called *The Inner Game of Tennis*, a very different kind of self-help tennis book in which the author, W. Timothy Gallwey, explains an approach to tennis from a Zen standpoint. When I read it, it seemed to me he described what I was searching for even though he did not seem totally aware of how absolutely critical this factor is. I believe it is critical not only to playing tennis but also to acquiring any other skill, and especially the skill of any positive addiction no matter what it may be. First, he describes the average tennis player as one who goes out onto the court and tries his best to play good tennis. If he is conscientious he takes some lessons, and if he doesn't take lessons he usually reads several books about tennis in an attempt to improve his game. The author states that even a good tennis player reaches his peak after a few years (maybe ten to twelve years for a pro), then his game, no matter what he tries to do through the usual lessons or books, never budges much past the peak he reached. Most players and many teachers accept that this peak is determined mostly by physical rather than mental limitations. They may struggle to improve past their peak—if they didn't, most teaching pros would go broke—but they don't really expect too much and almost always this turns out to be the case. In *The Inner Game* Gallwey suggests that athletes are more limited by their mental than by their physical stamina and skill. What he describes, after giving countless lessons, is student after student who seem to groove themselves into bad habits, and once grooved, the usual lessons do not help—in fact, too many may do harm.

In tennis the usual teacher goes through an endless patter of raise your backswing, lower your backswing, tighten your wrists, loosen your wrists, straighten your arm, bend your arm, step into the ball, step back from the ball, follow through, take your racquet back quicker, slower, further, watch your footwork—each lesson a huge dose of critical do's and dont's almost all to no avail.

When he observed that time after time his traditional instruction was ineffective he began to teach and advocate a totally different approach, which he calls Zen Tennis or the inner game. Rather than continually attempting to correct the errors of the complex series of motions that make a smooth tennis swing, motions that evidently don't lend themselves well to being broken down into their individual components and corrected, he asks his student just to try to hit the ball well and to think as little as possible of exactly what he is doing in the process. He advises him to watch his teacher or any other good player on the court or on television, not with any particular idea of copying him, but rather to observe him calmly and peacefully with the knowledge that what the expert does well will register in his, the student's, mind. He teaches his student through showing him, encouraging him, never criticizing him, and most of all he attempts to teach him *not to criticize himself.* He teaches him to observe where the ball goes and make a mental note of where he wants it to go next, and then to hit it without particularly concerning himself about his swing or footwork and especially about where he hit it the last time. The student concentrates more on where he wants to hit the ball than where he has hit it. If he can do this he will soon play better tennis.

Gallwey claims that we have to learn to play an existential

game, to take each shot for itself, *observing but not concerning ourselves with where the last shot went, good or bad.* We should try to develop a sense of detachment about everything except our immediate shot. We defeat ourselves through self-criticism and, rather than improving ourselves through the traditional way of trying to correct this or that and criticizing ourselves for not doing it, we lock ourselves into our final inadequate game.

What he points out—and from my observation it certainly seems to be true, both personally while attempting to play tennis and through watching professional athletes in many sports—is that at times the athlete seems to be playing "out of his head." In fact, that is the actual term observers use to describe an athlete like a basketball player on a streak who flings the ball in from all over the court, a tennis player who for several games seems to hit every shot perfectly, a football quarterback who hits pass after pass, usually at the end of a game, a baseball pitcher who seems almost unbeatable as he grooves the ball in exactly the right spot time after time, or a golfer who plays a relaxed and almost perfect round, sinking impossible putts and hitting unbelievable approaches. Gallwey says that when any good athlete is able to get himself into the "out-of-his-mind state" he is then able to play an almost perfect existential or Zen game. This state is not exclusive to athletes. Melissa Hayden, a ballet dancer, reached it at least once, she reported: "One night, dancing *Concerto Barocco,* a Balanchine work that epitomizes purity of movement and music, everything came together beautifully. My technique took over the steps; the orchestra was perfect; the tempos were inspired; the other dancers excelled themselves, and my partner and I worked together as one mind and body. I was not dancing. I was being transported, compelled to move by the music, and mystically moved by everything I had ever experienced and learned before, in my career and in my life. I have never been so exhilarated, exhausted, and fulfilled after a performance."* In her beautiful description of the PA state the mind flows with the body. The two cease completely to be antagonistic to each other and blend into one. Now the game or the dance is transformed into an emotion, a feeling of perfection that flows in waves of satisfaction from the player to the target or the dancer to the music without any of the self-critical interference that is ordinarily experienced. He then *plays over his head because he is out of his head.* When this happens the athletes are for those brief periods in a PA state. The very top athletes, never a large number in any sport, get into this PA state often and in it they intensely enjoy the game because besides the tangible satisfaction of their superior performance they get the further satisfaction of the highly desirable PA state of mind. Gallwey jokingly cautions that if you are ever up against this kind of competitor, to get him back "into his head" just ask him why he is playing so well. As soon as he thinks to answer, he will lose it; it is difficult to attain and a very fragile state.

Probably the reason many top athletes are where they are is that they do reach the state that not only remarkably enhances their physical skills but gives them the increased mental strength to deal with the stresses of competition. While there are other valuable concepts in *The Inner Game of Tennis* in terms of PA, I believe that the ability to become non-self-critical and at the same time try to improve (which seems to be, but in Zen is not, a contradiction in terms) is the *crucial factor* that makes it possible to reach the PA state regularly enough to become positively addicted. *Therefore, I believe that for anyone to go "out of his mind," to let his brain spin free in whatever activity he is in, physical or mental, he must*

*Melissa Hayden, "Wraparound," *Harper's Magazine* (December 1974), p. 9

learn to engage in the activity in a non-self-critical way.

Unfortunately, our whole upbringing and all of our schooling militate against our learning to do this. It is the rare child who is raised by example, patiently taught good behavior, and insulated from competition in his early years. Thus, in later life most people, even professional athletes, are not able to compete to try to win and remain noncritical of themselves for losing. Only the most competent people or, in athletics, the finest athletes ever reach this state and then usually only for brief periods, rarely for an extended time. To continue to use athletics as an example, I am sure that many athletes have the physical attributes to excel but few have developed the strength to be non-self-critical as they learn the skills. Therefore, they rarely reach the PA state in which the mind and body flow together and their performance peaks beyond belief. In fact, one of the differences between the top professional and the good athlete is that the professional has the strength not only to stand the pain of his own self-criticism, which because of the way he is taught he must endure on the way to the top, but also somehow or other to learn to rise above it as he continues. The reason that competitive sports are so draining, that so many athletes quit without ever reaching the top, or quit before they reach their peak, or quit the competition long before they physically have to (most commonly seen in golf, a highly self-critical game) is that they cannot stand the pain of the continual self-critical state they must endure when they compete and don't win. *This is why positive addiction activities, athletic or not, for most of us who don't have both great strength and top skill have to be noncompetitive.* Not only must we not compete with others, we must learn not to compete with ourselves if we wish to reach the PA state. That means even as we try to improve we must be careful not to criticize ourselves in the process. Now we can see why the runner in

Toronto turns away when another runner comes down the path and wants to run alongside him: he is aware that almost imperceptibly he will try to go a little faster, and in doing so risk being outrun. But even if he outruns the man who runs beside him he will be aware of the competition. As soon as this happens, unless he is the world's greatest runner, he will start to evaluate himself critically and any chance to reach the non-self-critical positive addiction state is lost. He will just run and get tired and even if he "wins" he loses because he will get much less pleasure from his run. That doesn't mean that runners can't run together; they can and do, but they have to run together in perfect harmony, in total accept-ance of each other, something runners perhaps more so than other athletes can occasionally do, but it is hard. They may enjoy a social run but they won't reach PA, so they usually do a joint run only once or twice a week. When they run seriously, which whether they know it or not is partly for positive addiction, they run alone.

Western man, who is raised to be competitive, to be con-cerned with winning, finds it very difficult not only not to compete with others but not to go into competition with himself, to set goals, to time himself, to keep close tabs on his self-improvement. In our culture these are all highly desir-able traits but traits which unfortunately seem to lead to high blood pressure and heart disease, especially when we have some difficulty reaching our self-set goals. Since these traits reduce the chances of reaching PA, running, for the self-critical person, will be a grind and hard to continue because he never "wins!" Only if he can learn to relax and flow along, to accept himself in what he is doing, to have confidence, will he eventually improve and be able to reach PA.* While it is

*See Joe Henderson, "Run Gently, Run Long," Booklet of the Month No. 37, *Runner's World* (July 1974).

difficult, many runners and meditators and others have learned to reach it, and as they enjoy themselves they gain strength.

Whether we wish to reach positive addiction or not it is difficult to overemphasize the importance of learning to be non-self-critical as much as we can all of our lives. This does not mean that it is desirable never to criticize ourselves, to blind ourselves to many inadequacies that can easily be corrected. In fact, self-evaluation and self-correction are the foundation of Reality Therapy. How we criticize ourselves, however, is vitally important because we must learn to direct our criticism at those activities which it is possible to correct; otherwise we will be too hard on ourselves and may lock ourselves into failure. For example, if you get a call to come home because your father is dying and you don't get there on time, it is self-destructive to spend the rest of your life criticizing yourself for something you can't correct. In the process you will lose strength and be less able to live your life effectively. But it is equally senseless to give up golf after a few bad rounds or drop out of college if you fail a critical course. In most instances there are ways you can improve if you are strong enough not to let the pain push you into irrational acts. If we are too critical we tend to press, to become too self-aware, to become rigid, all of which hurts, all of which reduces our performance, all of which tends to make us give up and, in doing so, lock ourselves into painful, miserable failure. The beautiful part of positive addiction is that whatever it is we ordinarily don't need it. It is an extra that we choose to do. No one needs to run by himself for an hour at six in the morning, rain or shine, but if we do, who would care about it except ourselves? Because of these criteria it is usually possible, though at times hard, because of our competitive upbringing, to be genuinely noncritical of ourselves during this and other PA activities. Even if we don't reach PA, which many of us never will, it is still important to have at least one activity that is all ours, in which we can accept ourselves completely. We may not reach PA but we will get a great deal of welcome peace and relaxation that we all need.

Finally, let me discuss love and sex because some people report this as a positive addiction for them. While in a good love relationship we should and usually do experience the PA state, I don't believe many of us experience it consistently enough or long enough for it to be addicting. There is a difference between a pleasurable biopsychological need and an addiction, and love and sex are much more the former than the latter. Love isn't addicting because love between mortals rarely exists for any period of time without criticism, which almost always results in self-criticism, usually quite a bit. While it isn't hard to remain in love, it is hard to keep the totally accepting attitude toward your lover that exists in the beginning. As most love relationships continue, each partner, having no one else, begins to find fault with the other. It may not be much—many relationships continue to grow and find new avenues for love, but few can continue in the pink glow of total acceptance in which they started. Therefore, as any love relationship continues, a little self-doubt and self-criticism arise and as they do the chances to spin out on sex and love regularly enough to become addicted decrease.

In the beginning of love there are usually traces of the PA state which add a pleasure component over and above what we ordinarily experience, and in any good relationship it continues to occur on special, warm occasions. Reunions, making up after spats, affairs, remarriages, all may provide some of the PA state but never on a regular enough basis to reach addiction. So while love is enjoyable, it is too tied to performance, which is necessarily judged by the standards of your loves. Since these standards are almost impossible to satisfy completely over any long period of time, I believe those who report love to be addicting are in the discovery state, not the holding state, which while enjoyable, rarely reaches the perfection of the beginning.

For these same reasons I believe it is almost impossible to become addicted to any activity that is in any way judged by others. Good friendships where the friends do not see each other too often and where there is no emotional, financial, or filial dependence may, when the friends get together, cause both to experience the PA state. Again, however, it does not occur frequently enough to be addicting. I am not so cynical as to believe that all friendships and all love are fleeting—far from it—but in the context of this discussion one can have long and deep relationships yet not reach addiction. Therefore, for all practical purposes, when we consider positive addiction in all its existing forms, it will be something you do alone. It does not depend on others.

three

THE PSYCHOLOGY OF STRENGTH AND WEAKNESS—THE POSITIVE ADDICTION STATE OF MIND AND WHY IT MAKES US STRONGER

In this chapter I will explain what I believe happens in our brains when we experience the PA state of mind and how we may gain strength through this experience. The best way to start is to take a close look at what makes strong people strong. I believe that their ability to find love and worth, when most of us would give up and settle for much less, is what separates the strong from the rest of us. All of us know some strong people personally. We know many more of them as the heroes and heroines of books, plays, and movies, both real and fictional. What they always seem to have that makes them strong is that no matter how many problems they face they rarely run out of options. Unlike the weak, who tend to give up and then choose symptoms to reduce their pain and perhaps later become addicted to get some pleasure in their lives, strong people never seem to be at the end of their rope. They almost never lock themselves into one pattern of thinking or behaving. Certainly they may be stymied or frustrated for a while, sometimes for quite a while, but even then they exercise an option which the weak consistently lack. This is the option to be patient, to wait, to stand pain and frustration for as long as it takes, because they are confident that they will eventually be able to figure some way out of their difficulty. Unlike the weak, the strong neither give up nor are driven by pain into rash or stupid behavior. They don't like pain any more than anyone else, but they are not willing to settle for short-term relief if it means reducing their options later. They don't rob Peter to pay Paul, they face reality now. While most of their strength has been gained through learning how to handle tough situations competently, it is most characteristic of the very strong that they also have the strength to take care of themselves in situations where they have neither experience nor support. It almost seems that they are endowed with the strength to figure out by themselves, with little or no help, what to do in new and completely strange situations. I believe this strength comes from the fact that they have implicit faith in the power of their brains. They have learned to rely on this complex thinking organ to solve hard problems, even problems for which there is no precedent. They may be helped by experience *but they don't depend on it and in many cases they don't seem to need it.*

I don't believe the strong are endowed with better brains than the rest of us; we all begin with about ten billion thinking neurons. What they have is a feeling of confidence, a feeling that no matter how tough things get there is always the possibility that somewhere in their brains a group of neurons will connect to form new neural pathways that will provide a thinking option to solve their problems. As I said before, they *feel* strong, more than they *know* they are strong, because no one, no matter how confident, can actually know his own future strength. In other words, while no one can actually know how many potentially usable neural paths he has, he can still have a strong pleasurable feeling or sense of confidence. It is this feeling, backed up over and over again by experience, that their brains will not let them down when times are hard, that sets the strong apart from the weak.

It is a very tangible feeling. When we have it we know we have it. We also are very much aware of when we don't have it, and it is something we can almost always sense in others. When we are in the presence of someone strong, if he is on our side, his strength is contagious; it gives us confidence too. Play tennis or bridge with a strong partner and see how quickly your game improves. Play against a strong team and the opposite often occurs. Sometimes it doesn't, however, as the strength is often contagious even when it is against us, challenging us to rise to the occasion. Another feature of the strong is charisma, but not all charismatic people are strong. If their charisma holds us for any length of time, however, it probably does stem from strength. Certainly people who have had a lasting influence upon their fellow men both at the time they lived and later, men like Lincoln and Churchill, women like Helen Keller and Eleanor Roosevelt, had both strength and charisma.

I believe that within the brains of the strong the ten billion neurons that we all have available to us are interconnected into many more pathways than most of us have. These pathways are not only greater in number and complexity but they are also more readily accessible to serve them than ours are to serve us. They are more accessible because strong people always have the confidence to accept themselves. Self-criticism and low confidence block us from our own brains. We have all experienced that block; when we are frightened or intimidated our minds go blank. It is so different from the easy flow of ideas that comes when we are self-accepting and confident. Since the number of ways ten billion neurons can connect is essentially infinite, it is unlikely we will ever be in such a tough situation that all of our potential neuronal hookups are exhausted. In every situation when man battles fate, as in plane crashes or shipwrecks, or when he battles man on the battlefield or in concentration camps, the strong have a much better chance of survival because they are able to create options in situations where none seem to exist. The classic cartoon showing two emaciated prisoners chained hand and foot high on a wall, one saying to the other, "Now here's my plan," is funny in a grim way to us, who would be optionless in their situation. All the speaker had going was his brain, but somewhere in his fertile brain he found a pathway.

Our strength, I believe, is proportional to the number of neuronal pathways hooked up and available to work for us when we call upon them. We start with a few genetic hook-ups—we learn a few things in our mother's uterus—but most of our lives the more we can give our brains a chance to grow, the stronger we will be. *The key to strength, much more strength than we ordinarily would have, is somehow to learn to create the optimal conditions for these new pathways to form within our brains.*

A recent example of a man who learned to do so and who survived almost solely through the strength of his own brain is Papillon. He told of his experience in the book titled with his name. He was able to figure out how to withstand an impossibly cruel solitary confinement because he was able to create a way to escape for long periods of time from his confinement into his own mind, into newly formed and continually forming vivid neuronal pathways of his own imagination. He was not crazy; he knew what he was doing and why he was doing it. He was more in touch with reality than those who couldn't do this, a process that not only sustained him but seemed to give him extra strength. Under less severe conditions most men would have died, not because of the physical deprivation, but because their brains are not strong enough. They would not have had the options needed to provide the confidence that it was worth the struggle to survive the conditions under which Papillon was forced to exist. He not only survived, he came out stronger. He had

65

many more options available to him when he emerged than when they locked him up. Strong people, therefore, develop more options to solve real problems they may not previously have faced, options they can call upon when times are hard. They also have a virtually inexhaustible supply of options in their own imaginations which come into play and sustain them when satisfactory behavior in the real world becomes impossible. When the real world is going well both the real and imaginary options provide the strong with a richness and zest in their lives that the weak never experience. Therefore, I believe, because they have more available pathways, strong people not only find more love and worth but they deal with what they find more enjoyably. They have a true zest for living because they are able to experience more possibilities in every situation both real and imaginary, and further, they are able creatively to blend the two. They are much less dependent than the weak on outside stimulation for entertainment and are rarely bored. Because there is more in their heads they live lives far beyond what a weaker person with fewer options can even imagine.

It also seems obvious that strength breeds strength, and as the pathways in their brains increase they probably do so at least geometrically, maybe even to a higher degree. Two pathways become four, four become sixteen, sixteen become two hundred and fifty-six. The more they have, the more they get. As long as they don't get self-critical—which is to the strong as bankruptcy is to the rich—they will get stronger at an increasingly rapid rate. The analogy that comes to mind to explain this explosive quality of gaining strength is that a strong man, under optimal conditions, has a brain like a complex electronic pinball machine, with all the high-scoring lights lit. Once these lights are on, every time a ball strikes a terminal the payoff explodes into a crescendo of points. The strong brain is, in the same sense, almost always lit up and waiting to be set off in a variety of ways. Each then becomes a starting point for many new ways, on and on, enormously expanding, but never coming close to utilizing the expansion potential available in the ten billion neurons we have been given.

If positive addiction makes us strong, as I claim it does, then the brain of a person who is positively addicted has more options than it had before he reached PA. What I believe happens, when the brain is allowed to spin free in the highly pleasurable PA state, is that during this time our neurons are, more than at any other time, free to hook up in new, different, and complex ways. It is the spinning-free, mentally relaxed PA state that *provides an extremely optimal condition for our brains to grow.* When we are directing our brains, as we do almost all the time in our everyday lives, they can grow only in the very selected area of whatever we are applying them to do. We call very strong direction concentration. It is efficient to concentrate, and when we do, we learn. In ordinary learning we create specific new pathways attached to that learning which we can call upon when we wish to use the knowledge. As we add these new usable pathways it feels good because it always feels good when we learn something we believe is worth learning. If it didn't feel good, we would have no incentive to learn, and without learning early man could not have survived, so this pleasure is a basic survival pleasure. It is a pleasure that now motivates most of us to want to continue to learn. This ordinary, direct learning is not addicting, however, because it just doesn't feel that good. It is too limited, too definite, too laborious, too unimaginative, too restricted, and unless our security is threatened we don't ordinarily suffer very much if we don't make an effort to learn a great deal. If we enjoy learning and we are deprived of a chance to learn—actually a highly unlikely situation because you can almost always learn—we may suffer a little, but nothing like the withdrawal from an addiction.

On the other hand, when the brain spins free there are no restrictions. Then the brain seems to have as an inherent function both the power and the will to grow by itself almost without bounds. If we are able to leave it alone, as we do in the PA state, it can grow more rapidly. It is almost like a cerebral Brownian movement. The neurons are set free like molecules in an unrestricted field to send out electrical or chemical feelers which then hook up into any possible pathway arrangement. Of course, since our brains have a reservoir of past experience and are always aware of present stress, initially when our neurons are set free, they will tend to arrange themselves in ways that will attempt to solve some of the stresses and strains of our past, present, and anticipated future. But as the time our brains are set free extends, allowing us to go deeper into the PA state, our neurons do far more than this. They go ahead on their own, calling on the remotest of stimuli past, present, and future, eventually going far beyond any stimulus and experience and moving into new, unused, "virgin" areas to arrange and rearrange themselves in ways that have nothing whatsoever to do with anything we have experienced. The experience of having been someplace before, when you were never there, an experience psychologists call *déjà vu,* is an example of being there first in your brain through a coincidental pathway, probably loosely based on some long-forgotten stimulus or association. Thus in the PA state, perhaps more than at any other time, our neurons hook up in totally new ways which may *prepare us and later enable us* to think creatively, write, compose, make scientific breakthroughs. It is in this state that we may develop the mental wherewithal to handle new, unexpected, and possibly overwhelming stresses and strains. We are strong because somehow or other a pathway that has newly formed can be called upon to do the job. I stress *prepare* because it is this *preparation experience, the expansion as these new paths are formed, whether they are used or not, that causes the PA state to feel so good.*

Einstein was a man who exemplified this kind of strength. He did not always think symbolically in language, signs, or symbols, as most of us are taught to do and do easily. Often he thought spatially, beyond symbols, delving into ideas that proved to be almost impossible to express within the finite bounds that limit most symbolic thinking. His early teachers thought he was dumb or lazy because there was no way he could communicate to them what was going on in his head. I believe he experienced much of this original thinking when he was in a natural PA state (his absent-mindedness is legendary) but it was difficult for him to be creatively absent-minded because his teachers were so critical of his symbolic ineptness. When they complained, his parents had the good sense to place him in a nontraditional school where he was encouraged, not criticized. Here he was accepted, and in a supportive, less structured, intellectual atmosphere he began to bloom. Had this not occurred, had he, as a student, never escaped from the tyranny of the pay-attention, symbol-limited teachers who naturally dominate our schools, he could easily have become so self-critical that he might never have gained access to the genius of his mind. I am sure there are others who think "differently" who are destroyed by the system that purports to educate them. The number may not be high but to lose an Einstein is a big price to pay for schools which tend too often to stifle the nonconforming, "absent-minded" student.

While I have emphasized the good feeling that accompanies the mind-expanding PA state, I don't want to suggest that this feeling is so extraordinary that all other good feelings pale beside it. Obviously, this is not true or positive addicts would devote all their time to their addiction, which they do not. A strong person enjoys many good feelings, most of them, I am sure, much more than the PA state, but I believe there is no pleasure that we ordinarily experience that is the same as the pleasure of the PA state. The difference is that when we feel good in the usual sense we can easily relate the feeling to what we are actively doing or what is going on around us. The feeling is tangible and understandable; *the pleasure is an active pleasure like sex or good food or winning an award,* pleasures all directly related to what is happening. The pleasure of anticipation, like betting on a horse, or the pleasure of dumb luck, like finding fifty dollars in the street, are all examples of the many possible pleasures that are obviously related to something we do or experience. Therefore, ordinarily, when we feel good we almost always know immediately or can soon figure out why we do.

The pleasure of the PA state is different. It is not directly related to anything tangible that we are doing or experiencing. It may accompany what we are doing—in positive addicts it always does—but even the positive addict can't make the PA state happen. His addiction is his attempt, usually successful, to provide the optimal conditions for it to happen, but the more he tries to get directly to the PA state the more it eludes him. Thus, while it feels good, it is not an active pleasure. It is passive, it is completely inside our brains. It seems to occur most when we are not thinking of anything or when what we are doing takes very little mental effort. *To repeat, we really can't make it happen; if we could, it would not be passive, it would be active.*

Even meditation, which is as close to a direct attempt to produce the PA state as we have, does not necessarily make it happen. It is like fishing—we can buy the right tackle and go where we are told there are fish, but we can't make the fish bite. Perhaps another way to describe it is this: when we do experience the particular pleasure of PA *essentially all that happens is the experience.* At the same time it is happening or later, because we have gained strength through its happening, *it can profoundly increase the effectiveness of what we do, and with it our active pleasures, but the PA state still remains passive.* In the case of the athlete who is playing "out of his head" it adds to his active enjoyment of the game because it markedly increases his performance. So while it may and usually does cause other feelings, activities, and experiences to be more intense, it, itself, remains mysteriously separate as an intensely pleasurable but passive, internal, "in-our-head" experience.

As I have indicated, the PA state is not exclusive to positive addiction. It happens to almost all of us at times. It can accompany love or sex, or be part of the afterglow of any great achievement. I am sure mountain climbers get it when they reach the summit. Any time we are relaxed, satisfied, and noncritical it may happen, until we get going again and interrupt it. As good as it may feel, not only don't we ordinarily know how to create the conditions for it to occur, we usually don't even think about trying to make it happen. We accept it, we enjoy it, but we usually don't separate it from our active pleasures; in fact, we rarely recognize it for what it is. When it happens we may even describe this additional, in-the-head pleasure as a peak experience, to use A. H. Maslow's term, as did Melissa Hayden, but in its "natural occurring state" it is not consistently reproducible.

For example, sometimes when making a speech to a responsive audience, right in the middle of presenting an idea I pause a moment, maybe just one second. I don't really know why I pause but I feel as if something has come free in my head. It feels good but the whole experience is almost imperceptible. When this happens my speech doesn't change much except it gets a little more relaxed, a little more free, a little more pleasant for me and the audience. Sometimes nothing more happens but sometimes there suddenly flashes into my mind a new and previously unthought-of idea or train of ideas, which are not always but are often very pertinent to what I am talking about. If they are unrelated I blot them out, but when they are related they often open up possibilities I never thought of before. Where they come from I don't know. They seem to come out of nowhere and they surprise me, because some of the subjects I have talked about for years were, I believed, ideologically exhausted. Less often, but sometimes at the same time as what I have just described is happening, or at a different time, something similar yet not the same occurs. I feel that while I am talking I have suddenly left my speech. I've gone away. Not far away because I can still hear my speech going on (and it is usually going well) but for a while, sometimes for minutes at a time, my head is someplace else. I get a confident, powerful, often humorous feeling, a pleasurable urge to laugh and joke and sometimes I hear the jokes break through. The jokes are in context but I don't know where they came from. It is as if my "main" mind is now listening and my "other" mind takes over the talk, and for the lack of a better term, "I wing it." I start to spin out right in the process of talking, a whole series of new ideas starts to flow, and I talk "out of my head." It doesn't happen often but it happened once in the fall of 1974 for over an hour. It was a true peak experience. I am not addicted to public speaking but I like to talk perhaps more than anything else, both for the tangible pleasure of a responsive audience, and also for the intangible PA occasions I have just described. It occurs only when I have a highly responsive audience, an audience that is almost totally noncritical of what I have to say. If I have that, and if I am relaxed and feel confident, and if I have plenty of time, it may happen. In the past year it has happened so often that I can feel it coming and, as I said, when it comes I give a far better speech than I ordinarily do. Evidently I need the noncritical audience there to encourage me to spin off into this state. When I have a nonresponsive or critical audience, when I am pushed for time or overtired, I labor and my speech is not nearly as good.

When I write, it may also happen but not as often. I try not to criticize myself very much but it's difficult. I am also very sensitive about showing someone else my writing because if they criticize it, then I won't be able to get this feeling with this piece of writing for a long time, maybe never. But the sensitivity, even if I don't show my writing to anyone, is a form of self-criticism which I am sure stops the PA state. Once something I have newly written is criticized, unless I have great faith that the critic is trying to help me and that I can correct what I am writing, it seems to close me up, to lock me away from my ideas. Because even flashes of this PA state are valuable to my writing, I work on what I am writing for a long time before I show it to anyone. By that time, I hope I have gained enough confidence in what I have written so I will be slightly less sensitive. No matter how successful you are, creativity is a very fragile business. You need the PA state desperately in order to free your mind to create, but you also need some support from others to keep going. Since you can't, in creative writing, produce much more than gibberish in the first drafts, you are caught between the desire to get a pat on the back to keep yourself going and the risk, if you don't get it, to burden yourself with doubt. Once the seed of doubt is planted, you can forget about the PA state, it won't accompany this particular effort for a long time, maybe never.

To introspect a little further, when I speak I am like a professional athlete who occasionally plays out of his head. But if I try to make it happen, if I try to be too creative or make a conscious attempt to be funny, I never even begin to reach this particular state. The very act of "being creative" effectively blocks the process. This block must drive professional comics bananas because only when they are able to rise above their canned jokes can they really get into humor. Yet if they deviate from the script they may lay an egg that will prevent the PA state from occurring and only in the PA state can they reach their peak. I enjoy making an audience laugh but I am glad I don't have to be funny. It is the strain to reach this peak regularly that must make clowns so sad. I do, however, try to create the conditions for it to happen by preparing as much as I can. I learn my subject inside out but I make no effort to compose the actual talk. For the past ten years I have even totally stopped using notes. I sit down to relax both myself and the audience (I have found it almost never happens if I talk standing up), and as soon as I can (the start of a talk is always rough) I try to just let the talk "happen." Then if everything else is right and if the talk starts to "happen," sometimes the PA state occurs and then it all gets better. It is like forgetting something and then trying to recall it and feeling as if it's on the tip of your tongue. If you can relax and let your mind go, suddenly as if from nowhere, the memory emerges. In speaking before an audience the PA state emerges for me in the same way.

Obviously, then, to get into the maximum PA state what you have to do is know your subject well and then have faith that your mind will do what you have confidence it can do.

This is very hard to do. Your mind wants to be involved. Following our old ethic of work hard, don't relax, make sure all the bases are touched, you feel a twinge of guilt if you do what I say. You have been told to keep your eye on the ball for so long you can't take it off. But if, as I sometimes do, you can get into the PA state, you will do better. This is maybe one of the differences between a pro and an amateur. The pro keeps his eye on the ball but he lets his mind go. This is why Jimmy "the Greek" Snyder, who sets the odds in Las Vegas, goes with experience in a championship game and he is usually right. The old pros don't push, they let it happen; they know they have the stuff, and given a little time it will happen. The World Series of 1974, where the experienced Oakland A's easily beat the youthful L. A. Dodgers (who tensed up and beat themselves), clearly showed this to be true. If you are competent in anything and you can let your brain spin free while you are doing it, you will experience both more competence and more pleasure than if you keep your brain tightly controlled by conscious effort. The ordinary competent brain is like a well-trained dog on a leash, dutifully following you where you take it but with all the excitement of a leashed dog held to his master's heel. The PA brain is like a trained dog who is trusted by his master for a while off the leash—it runs off into a whole new world of ecstatic freedom taking you and your competence with it, pushing you to new heights and new experiences.

Strong people, regardless of whether they are positively addicted or not, are able to do this regularly in one way or another. Probably the stronger they are the more they are able to unleash their minds in a variety of different ways. This is an important reason why they are strong and why they usually continue to get stronger. If, along the way, they figure out how to gain the PA state regularly, even if they are not aware of exactly what is happening, they usually become addicted to the process. If they are deprived of this habit they suffer discomfort, but it takes them a while to learn that the discomfort is a withdrawal pain because they are deprived of the PA state. After a while most do understand and they accept their addiction because they sense how valuable it is for them. They may not talk much about it for fear of seeming odd but they become aware of the process.

The concept that the PA state occurs in strong people and

probably serves to make them stronger is soundly supported by an article published in the *New York Times Magazine,* January 26, 1975, entitled "Are We a Nation of Mystics?" The authors are Andrew M. Greeley and William C. McCready, sociologists and Roman Catholic priests. In a different way and a different context they have done some remarkable research to support my conclusions in this chapter about the PA state. In the beginning they cite two such PA-state experiences which they call mystical. John Buchan, a novelist and governor general of Canada, wrote of an experience that happened to him in Africa as he bathed in a clear, cool spring in the Kalahari called Malmani Oog:

> Then and there came on me the hour of revelation, when though savagely hungry, I forgot about breakfast. Scents, sights and sounds blended into a harmony so perfect that it transcended human expression, even human thought. It was like a glimpse of the peace of eternity.

F. C. Happold, a contemporary of Buchan sitting in his room at Cambridge, on the first of February 1913, wrote:

> I was overwhelmingly possessed by Someone who was not myself, and yet I felt I was more myself than I had ever been before. I was filled with an intense happiness, and almost unbelievable joy, such as I had never known before and have never known since. And over all was a deep sense of peace and security and certainty.

The authors go on to say:

> But wherever the place and whatever the trigger and whoever the person, there run through the accounts of such interludes certain common themes—joy, light, peace, fire, warmth, unity, certainty, confidence,

rebirth. Easterner and Westerner, saint and sinner, man and woman, young person and old, all seem to report a virtually identical experience—intense, overpowering joy which seemed literally to lift them out of themselves (in some instances the ecstatics thought they could actually see themselves from the outside).

The authors began to think that these were not unusual experiences even though they had been reported as such. They wondered if they did not occur to many people but were extremely surprised at the large number of people who reported a PA-state (mystical) experience similar to those recounted above. In order to research their belief they decided to take a poll. They used a religious base for their question, which I believe tends to distort the answers slightly, but when they began their study they believed that these were religious experiences. They asked fifteen hundred people, "Have you ever had the feeling of being close to a powerful spiritual force that seemed to lift you out of yourself?" About six hundred persons, two-fifths of the fifteen hundred persons asked, reported having at least one such experience. About three hundred said they had it several times and seventy-five said they had it often; some of the latter, I would suspect, were positive addicts. To be fair, the authors do attempt in the article to be objective, and even though they asked the question from a religious base they don't claim that the experience is necessarily religious. They say:

> We are then dealing with people who report an intense experience of being lifted out of themselves by a powerful spiritual force. More than this we cannot say. Even if some (many, most) of these experiences are not "mystical" [religious] in the classic sense of the word, it is nonetheless a striking phenomenon that a large segment of the population is prepared to report such an intense experience. Whatever the nature of that experi-

ence, and however much it might fit the definition of traditional mysticism, it is in itself worth investigating.

Even with this mild disclaimer that all the experiences are not classically religious they do retain this idea throughout the article. If we can look at these experiences as neither religious nor necessarily produced by an outside force, then the article makes good sense as an independent research into the PA state.

Those who responded positively to this question were for the most part advantaged people in our society. They were well off economically and were mostly college educated. Almost all of them reported happy recollections of their childhood, close relations between their mothers and fathers and between themselves and each of their parents, which would make them non-self-critical and set the stage for these experiences. They also reported a religious approach by their fathers and mothers that was characterized by joyousness in contrast to the sin-dominated religion that makes it difficult for people to accept themselves. The authors present an extremely significant finding about their mental strength:

> There is nothing on the surface, then, which would indicate that, either socially or psychologically, the ecstatics are deprived or disturbed. . . . We did administer the brief Psychological Well-Being Scale developed by Prof. Norman Bradburn. The relationship between frequent, ecstatic experiences and psychological well-being was .40, the highest correlation, according to Bradburn, he has ever observed with this scale. We tried to explain away or at least diminish the strength of this correlation by taking into account the number of variables. . . . The result was that the correlation remained virtually unchanged, declining only from .40 to .39.

Here we have not proof but strong evidence from another source that if people have even limited PA-state experiences they score very high on a test of psychological well-being or, in my terms, psychological strength. When the authors reported this finding to their professional colleagues in mental-health work they were rejected with the statement that these people couldn't be having religious experiences. Like me, the social scientists didn't believe in the religious aspect of this PA-state experience, but, unlike me, they tended to disbelieve the whole concept. This caused the authors to reduce their claim that these were exclusively religious experiences, and honestly say:

> Maybe not [maybe they are not religious experiences], but they are having something; and whatever the hell it is they are having, it correlates with mental health at a very high level. If we had found any other correlate, the mental-health establishment would be knocking down our doors demanding to know more. If anything else but "ecstasy" were that good for you it would sell as if it wouldn't be on the market next year.

Finally they say they have no explanation why the experiences are always joyous except a religious one that unusual forces are felt by the person as gracious and benign. This may be so, but I think a better explanation is that the process of one's brain expanding in new directions, plus gaining access to pathways that were previously denied, is like getting out of jail and finding treasure. The analogy that comes to mind is the joy of Edmond Dantès when he discovered the treasure on the island of Monte Cristo. I would urge that this *Times* article be read. It contains more than I can adequately describe here.

Whether you are addicted or not, it is my assumption that

the key to the whole process of gaining mental strength through positive addiction is self-acceptance to the point where you are able to leave your brain alone long enough to experience the PA state. The less you are able to leave your mind alone the less it will reach its potential. You may not have the intense mystical experience described by Greeley and McCready in the *New York Times* article but most of us have had at least flashes of these experiences in short periods of time when we were very accepting of ourselves and other conditions were right. If we are too self-critical, we have to learn to get along with only the options we learn directly, which leaves us deprived of a great deal of our potential strength. Since it is characteristic of the weak to criticize others or complain a lot, both of which quickly end up as self-criticism, the weaker they are the less they experience the PA state. Without it they have fewer options, so it is also characteristic of the weak that they use these fewer options over and over. Since happiness ordinarily demands much more strength than these overused and inadequate pathways can provide, the weak are less successful in their quest for love and worth and they hurt.

Weakness, which is almost always associated with pain, is the exact opposite of strength. The weak person has few options or has little access to the ones he has, which amounts to the same thing. As explained in Chapter One, when a person learns through experience that he can't find the love or worth that he would like to have, the pain tells him to get going and try harder, to consider a new approach, do something. Unfortunately, because he is weak, his options are limited and he quickly runs out of new approaches. He usually ends up trying one or two ways to get what he wants over and over again as if no other choices were possible. You see this in weak children trying to amuse themselves. They try once or twice, give up, and then get upset and begin to cry, which is their symptomatic way of asking for help. Later in life they may complain that their marriage is unhappy, job no good, house inadequate, the weather bad, their family unappreciative, complaining continually but doing little else.

The constant griping and complaining that is characteristic of the weak drives the people around them crazy. As this happens, the stronger withdraw, leaving the weak person with less love and less chance for someone to believe he is worthwhile, effectively compounding his inadequacy. Nothing is more characteristic of a patient seeking psychiatric help than to complain bitterly and say, "I don't know what to do. I can't seem to do anything, doctor. Help me, I'm so miserable." Such people feel helplessness and pain because, in contrast to the strong, it is each neuron for itself within their brains. Theirs is a mental house divided against itself. Few of their neurons work well together and what hookups they have are either overused or, because of their self-criticism, unavailable to them. But if there aren't enough options available so they can reasonably remedy the situation, the pain they suffer, rather than serving as a stimulus, becomes a dead end. They know this. They know they are stuck with the pain so they use what energy they have, which even in the weak may be considerable, in trying to get rid of the pain. They try to turn off the clanging of their own alarm because they know they can't put the fire out. At least if they can get the alarm turned off they can burn in peace. In effect, they give up in an effort to reduce the pain. They try to renounce the love and worth they need in an effort to stop the pain that is pouring into their brains.

In Chapter One I explained that this first choice works only for a while. Because the weak can't give up on what they need, the pain returns. Like an active pleasure, *this is an active pain.* It is directly related to the lack of love and worth in their lives. They clearly understand the cause of the pain;

that is why they give up. The active pain of giving up may be exactly the same as the pain of a second-choice symptom. For example, we may be depressed when we give up and we may suffer later from the symptom of depression. *It is the same kind of pain but the difference is that when it is a symptom we less and less relate the pain to what we gave up.*

Except in rare instances like going completely crazy or acting out successfully, all symptoms hurt. They don't hurt any differently but they hurt less because now the suffering is not felt as the lack of love and worth. We are now too "sick" to "worry" about what we really need. The suffering is no longer active, it is now passive; it is now more and more "in the head." The pain may be depression, tension, fear, anxiety, or psychosomatic disability. These can occur by themselves, they can accompany a psychotic state, or they can quickly happen to a person acting out if he is stopped. In any case, as much as this passive, in-the-head pain may hurt, because it protects us from our inadequacy and allows us to ask for help, it doesn't hurt as much as the active pain that we tried to reduce by giving up. Because these symptoms are in our heads they tend at first partially, and later, if they persist, completely to mask our need for love and worth, so that when we ask for help it is rarely help to restore love and worth, but only help to stop the in-the-head, passive pain of the symptom. The reason the symptom always hurts, even though it hurts less, is that it would be against our survival if symptoms did not hurt. If we were able to convert weakness, inadequacy, and the loss of love and worth into good feelings we could not have survived as a race. That's *why* the symptom hurts, but *how it hurts, how it causes pain, is because it is essentially a one-track-brain experience.* It is an attempt to use one small set of pathways over and over until these literally begin to hurt from overuse. You use the depression pathway, the anxiety pathway, the fear pathway over and over until your brain literally reacts with pain at the friction caused by this overloading of a small number of paths. When a symptomatic person says he has a headache or his head feels funny he is telling the truth. His head does truly hurt because of his in-the-head pain. No matter how hard we try to get him off the track and back to using his brain to find love and worth, he resists, because this passive pain is better than the active pain he knows will return if he tries to face a reality he is too weak to handle.

This is why in psychotherapy we must make a relationship with him to help him to reexperience a degree of love and friendship that he has given up or to make plans with him so he can again experience worth, usually both. If we can do that, then we can begin to break him away from his overused symptom pathway and get him back into the rest of his mind. Then with more psychotherapy he may be able to find an option to gain more love and more worth and begin to feel some active pleasure, maybe enough tentatively to give up his symptom. This is why we must treat him as noncritically as possible so that he can accept himself and gain more access to his mind. We may not ever be able to be his best friend or provide anywhere near the love he needs—that would be unrealistic. We can, however, be enough of a non-critical friend to help him begin to figure out some options to solve his problems. He has the mental wherewithal; we have to help him to use it and get more.

Of course, we might at times be critical of him, but this is technique and, except for brief sections, this is not a book on psychotherapy. If we do use criticism as a technique we must be sure not to criticize what he cannot easily correct. We might criticize his appearance but we wouldn't criticize his failure in school or at work. We wouldn't even criticize his appearance unless we were sure we could help him plan to look better. The point, however, is that a symptom is an attempt to substitute a passive, in-the-head pain for an active, failure pain because it hurts less. To this extent symptoms work but they still hurt. Depression, as we all know, hurts like hell. Nevertheless, because they fear an increase in pain, people won't give up a very painful symptom unless they can move ahead, through help, to love and worth or *backward, further into their heads, by choosing to become negatively addicted, the third choice of the weak.*

People who make the third choice, the choice to try to become addicted, usually succeed. They succeed because an addiction has the peculiar quality not only of getting rid of the passive pain of the symptom (and what little active pain may coexist with it) but of replacing it with an intense but passive pleasure. Why alcohol, heroin, food, and gambling do this is not known, but there is no doubt that they do. My theory is that all the addictions have the power to set the weak, limited, passively painful brains of those who choose symptoms temporarily free. Under the influence of their negative addictions they experience the PA state of mind, only now this state is produced chemically or through food or gambling. It is the same state of mind—addicting—that occurs in a positive addiction, but it is reached in a much different way. When this happens regularly, the negative addict is born. The negative addicting process uniquely causes a quick surge of passive pleasure as his brain suddenly expands, usually under the influence of drugs, to the PA state. He experiences a surge of pleasure that not only blots out the passive pain but replaces it with what he describes as an ecstatic high. It is this feeling of intense but in-the-head, passive pleasure—which the alcoholic, for example, cannot get with anything else except alcohol—that quickly overwhelms him. If he continues he is hooked.

There is, however, a world of difference between the nega-

tive addict and the positive addict, both of whom *experience the PA state of mind. The negative addict experiences only the passive pleasure.* He does not experience the additional, active, tangible pleasure of the positive addict, who, unlike the negative addict, uses the strength gained through his PA state to get more from his life. With this strength, immediately or later, he pursues the active pleasure of finding more love and worth and succeeds. The negative addict *settles* for the relief from the passive pain provided by the surge or "rush" plus the several hours of passive pleasure that quickly follow. Because his brain is temporarily free he may feel strong enough in his addicted state, at least in the beginning of his addiction, to consider trying for love and worth. This is why drugs fool people in the beginning. Freud once thought that the PA state of mind produced by cocaine was the panacea of psychiatry. An addict soon realizes, and correctly, that since he hasn't had love or worth for a long time they won't come quickly or easily for him; he also feels a new euphoric strength that lets the possibility of getting them again at least cross his mind. He soon discovers, however, that even to begin to duplicate the intense passive pleasure he knows he can always get from his addiction with active pleasure he would need an almost instantaneous huge dose of love and worth. But to get a quick, pain-relieving surge of love or worth is rare even for the strong, and for the addict it is impossible. If, however, in his euphoria he decides to try for love and worth he necessarily must reduce his concentration on his addiction. He can't pursue love or worth while he is stoned, standing at the crap table, or stuffing his obese body with food. If, however, he is still determined, he finds himself unprepared for the sudden resurgence of pain both physical and mental. He quickly discovers that his brain is set free only for the short period of time that he can remain under the influence; as it wanes he begins to hurt. Therefore, in any negative addiction the strength the addict feels is of no permanent use in his life because it never lasts long enough or is strong enough for him to get quickly the amount of active pleasure from love or worth he needs to counteract the passive pain of his recent existence. Besides, he has no good place to start because he has given up and has been without love or worth for a long time. He has little chance to find them in the brief periods his addiction may set him free to look.

What he does, however, is use whatever strength his addiction provides to further his addiction. In his term, "he takes care of business." He does this because he learns quickly through experience how brief and fleeting his pleasure is. When the addiction wears off, the PA state abruptly terminates, causing the brief increase in pathways quickly to constrict back to the painful grooves of his symptom. As his brain constricts or rapidly contracts, not only do all thoughts of love and worth disappear, but he hurts even more than before he was addicted because now he experiences *the added active pain of withdrawal.*

I believe that he actually feels his brain suddenly contract as the addiction wears off, and this sudden contraction from spinning free to the limited pathways of his symptom choice is excruciating. It is much more painful than if he had never felt the pleasure of the expansion and he becomes desperate to reexperience his addiction in order to reexpand his mind, both to stop the pain and renew the pleasure. The only pathways in the addict that remain strong and seem to get stronger the longer he is addicted are the newly formed and forming options which he can call upon to pursue the certain pleasure of his habit. In its pursuit, driven by pain and the promise of pleasure, he develops ferocious unilateral strength. He gives everything else up. He may allow his body and social position to deteriorate completely because he doesn't care that much about them. All he cares for is the limited world of his addiction. Here he is often a creative genius.

In the quest for his addiction he may even seem to pursue love and worth, but on close examination this is only a pseudo-pursuit. He does so only if he can use people or power to further his habit. Many a person married to an addict or employing one can testify to the truth of this statement. The addict will victimize almost anyone in his effort to get his high —he may do a superb job for his employer and at the same time steal him blind—but do so with such psychopathic charm that those who are victimized are often puzzled that they don't dislike the addict more. The only way an addict will truly pursue love and worth again is to give up his addiction, and to an addict that door is closed. No one knows it is closed more than he because he chose to close it and he will never open it until he kicks his habit. But by himself, a negative addict hasn't the strength to kick.

Further, and unfortunately for him, the habit itself gradually becomes less effective. The dose of drug he takes to cause his mind to spin free and expand must be increased. The drugs will still relieve the pain through the surge—they never grow so ineffective that they won't do this—but the following pleasure diminishes, perhaps because his mind has been up and down so many times in the same way. This does not mean he will quit; it is the only game in town for him, but it just doesn't work as well. With the increased dose his pleasure increases but there is a limit to which any addiction will take him. He may never grow tolerant of gambling, as many successful workaholics prove, but he will run out of money if he is a Las Vegas-type gambler because there isn't enough money in the world to satisfy the habit of an addicted gambler. Food will also work less and less as the food addict becomes grotesquely obese and sick. If it is drugs, in some cases he overdoses, in others he gets sick from contaminants, and in many cases of heroin addiction, the struggle to get the money to satisfy his increasing need becomes too much even for his strength and he reaches his limit.

At this point most addicts, usually drug addicts, will have enough strength to deprive themselves of the drug or let others do it for a short time in order to reduce the tolerance their own brains have developed. In a short time they can get back to the point where less of the drug can set their minds free. They are willing to suffer temporary withdrawal, the lesser of two evils, in order to reduce the hassle necessary to get enough drugs to renew the pleasure of their addiction.

Drugs, food, and gambling provide pleasure to many more people than addicts but to most of us they are not addicting. The reason they are not is that nonaddicts don't have the intense pain that addiction relieves. We enjoy the mild expansion of our minds, the passive, peaceful pleasure that small doses of the drug or behavior provide, but we would rather get our pleasure actively. We have no intention of settling for the passive pleasure that is all the addict can hope to get. Besides, we don't have the constant pain so we don't need large doses of the drug to provide the rush, the surge of pleasure that the addict needs desperately.

Since nonaddicts too use plenty of drugs you might wonder if they gain strength from the limited PA state of mind that their addiction induces. Most of them don't take enough alcohol, the main drug they use, to get into the PA state very deeply. But even if they do, their experience is the same as in addicts. The PA state is temporary—they are intoxicated while in it so they are ineffective, and as it wears off they suffer as their brains mildly "contract." This is felt mentally as depression or physically as a hangover-type headache. So in the nonaddict, if the positive addiction state is gained through a drug, the most it usually provides is a little relaxation, a spot of mental freedom that is eventually paid for in the slight withdrawal state. If the use of the "drug" is mild—a few drinks, an occasional huge meal, or a little friendly gambling—there is almost no withdrawal price to pay. The pleasure is genuine but does not provide any marked increase in strength because the PA effect is so small. Here I should mention cigarettes and coffee again. Both provide tiny but very consistent PA experiences; neither is strong enough to do more than give a little pleasure or relief from tension that both addicts and nonaddicts enjoy. The negative addictions which to the weak can easily become their whole lives, to the reasonably strong become a mild pleasure, a relief from the tension of the day, a way to free the brain socially for short periods, but these stronger people are not about to settle for only this passive pleasure. They still mostly want the active pleasure of love and worth which they must seek independently of this slight PA experience.

I have already explained the withdrawal pain of a negative addict; here I would like to attempt to explain the withdrawal pain of PA. As I will describe more fully in the following chapters, positive addicts do suffer withdrawal but I don't think very much of it comes from the contraction of their brains. Since they are able to leave their brains alone naturally, they are in a sense reexperiencing in their addiction a natural mental strengthening pattern. Thus, the pathways they form they keep, adding to their strength. They may move out of PA naturally, a process much different from the wrenching effect of a chemical wearing off. In addition, positive addicts are not returning to the painful symptom state of the negative addict which compounds his withdrawal. A further clue, if one studies their responses carefully, is that their suffering is not immediate. It takes a while, sometimes several days, in contrast to the negative addict, who begins to suffer as soon as his addiction diminishes, even while he is still under its effect.

Even so, most positive addicts claim to suffer quite a bit, and I believe that their suffering is a realistic response to the loss of a very pleasurable and easily obtained experience to which they have grown accustomed. They don't want to lose the regular passive pleasure of the PA state which they have come to expect. They suffer less than negative addicts because this pain is partly balanced by the fact that their lives are stronger, their active pleasures more intense. However, regardless of how strong we are, when we lose a regular, expected, and unique pleasure we want it back and the withdrawal pain we feel is our message to ourselves to get it back.

We probably suffer proportionately to the amount of time we are able to achieve the PA state. The more we achieve it the more we suffer—in fact, it is this withdrawal pain more than anything else that lets us know we've reached PA. Our suffering is increased because we know we can do something legal and beneficial which will so easily relieve the pain. Besides, we are well aware that PA is only helpful and to give it up is silly. It is like giving up shoes. You could probably walk barefoot the rest of your life, but why? The positive addict's brain is well aware of the pleasure it is missing and equally aware of how easily he can get this pleasure back, so naturally it reacts with a lot of misery. If for some reason he can't continue his habit he will try to find some substitute that is close. A runner can ride a bike or turn to yoga if his ankles get weak (as a heroin addict can turn to alcohol). Neither, however, is as satisfactory as the original it replaced. Therefore, while positive addiction is in some ways analogous to negative addiction, the depth of the withdrawal is never as severe. If the positive addict has to stop he will probably always miss it (this is characteristic of all addictions negative or positive) but he won't suffer as long or as severely as a negative addict because he withdraws to strength not weakness. If you are a positive addict and if for some reason you have to quit, be prepared to suffer, but also be prepared to be stronger than before you started. The suffering will eventually stop, the extra strength will never be lost.

four

THE SIX STEPS TO A POSITIVE ADDICTION

While I was having a discussion on positive addiction with a group of educators in May 1974, a woman of about thirty-five stood up and said that she was addicted to bicycle riding. She explained that every evening after supper, usually between six and seven, she rode her bicycle for an hour by herself around her neighborhood. Having not yet arrived at the concept of the PA state, I was mostly concerned with the discomfort she felt if she didn't ride her bike, so I asked her, "What happens if you don't ride your bike?" She replied, "Nothing happens, because I always ride my bike." Her statement was so definite that I asked her in a teasing way, "Well, what if one of your children were very sick and needed care, wouldn't you skip your bike ride?" Her half-humorous, half-serious reply was, "They better not get sick during the hour after dinner that I ride my bike." She stated something that I have since heard from almost everyone who has a positive addiction: the time they have set aside for whatever they do that they are addicted to is sacrosanct. They want neither the pain nor the loss of pleasure that accompanies skipping their habit. Exactly how they feel will be discussed in much more detail in the following chapters on meditators and runners, the two largest categories of positive addicts.

Perhaps meditators and runners are to positive addiction as heroin users and alcoholics are to negative addiction, in that these practices, positive or negative, provide the easiest or the most satisfactory pathways to the PA state, which as I explained in the preceding chapter is the core of all addiction. With this in mind, let's take a brief look at some other possible positive addictions with the understanding that there may be more than these examples. Remember, a positive addiction can be anything at all that a person chooses to do as long as it fulfills the following six criteria: (1) It is something noncompetitive that you choose to do and you can devote an hour (approximately) a day to it. (2) It is possible for you to do it easily and it doesn't take a great deal of mental effort to do it well. (3) You can do it alone or rarely with others but it does not depend upon others to do it. (4) You believe that it has some value (physical, mental, or spiritual) for you. (5) You believe that if you persist at it you will improve, but this is completely subjective—you need to be the only one who measures that improvement. (6) The activity *must* have the quality that you can do it *without criticizing yourself. If you can't accept yourself during this time the activity will not be addicting.* This is why it is so important that the activity can be done alone. Any time you introduce other people you chance introducing competition or criticism, often both. Risking criticism can be detrimental to the PA state, which is why many positive addicts keep quiet about what they do. Though my questionnaire did not inquire specifically about this point, it was volunteered by quite a few respondents and was perhaps best stated by one woman who discovered a form of meditation on her own:

> For a long time I did not discuss it [meditation] with anyone because I feared it was some kind of psychotic experience, mental disorder . . . or if not, at least it

would certainly sound like it to another. I no longer feel this way. I live a productive and good life and wonder why everyone doesn't use this gift which I am convinced all have access to but few ever use.

Even if you follow all of the six criteria for positive addiction there is absolutely no guarantee that you will succeed in becoming addicted. To become addicted you have to reach the PA state on a regular basis at least several times a week for several minutes to an hour each time. If this happens, then you experience a surge of pleasure which you learn to crave. If you deny yourself the PA activity for as little as three or four days you will suffer fairly severe withdrawal pain both physical and mental. As I will describe in detail in Chapter Six on meditation, many meditators as well as many others who fulfill the six criteria do gain strength from their practice but they don't reach addiction. If they continue they may eventually become addicted and gain much more strength, but most meditators are not positive addicts. They may experience brief flashes of the PA state but not enough so they suffer any significant withdrawal. Mostly what they achieve is a pleasant, relaxing habit which many of the respondents have erroneously reported as addiction. Although it doesn't happen often, it is possible to become addicted to any physical or mental activity by fulfilling the six criteria. I would like to describe some of the practices that people have reported as positive addictions, again with the caution that just because they are reported as PA does not make them so. My estimate is that of all the reported positive addictions, running, yoga, and meditating are the only practices in which people reach PA in significant numbers.

There are, therefore, two major categories of PA—the physical, led by the runners, and the mental, dominated by the meditators (yoga can be part physical and part mental).

Each is important enough to devote a following chapter to its practice. Responding to my inquiry into PA, many people filled out questionnaires in which they stated they were addicted to some particular practice. Under the mental practices, people have responded that they daydream and have also mentioned that it was a relief to have this practice verified as beneficial. As adults they have had difficulty admitting to this practice because daydreaming is something that you are supposed to do only as a small child and, unfortunately, even then not too much. Closely allied to meditating and daydreaming are a large group of routine, nontaxing physical activities, which I classify as mental because they can be done for long periods with almost no effort or conscious concentration. Examples of these are knitting, crocheting, needlepoint, tatting. Another group responds that gardening is their PA. One woman says, "Every day I mess around with houseplants and suffer if I skip a day." Quite a few people report that their PA is writing in a personal journal. Creative writing might possibly be addicting for great writers like Hemingway, who wrote regularly each morning from six to ten, but it is too self-critical an activity to be addicting to the nonprofessional. On the other hand, keeping a journal is a highly non-self-critical activity (if it weren't no one could endure the pain) and those who do it say that their minds frequently spin off as they record their day's activities, thoughts, and feelings. One woman says she is addicted to taking baths, three baths a day in which she sits and drifts in the warm water, not washing, just soaking up the aloneness of her warm, pleasant, self-taught meditatory experience. She too was grateful that the PA concept helped her to understand a habit she knew was good but was hesitant to talk about. One woman says that she is addicted to grooming herself and to applying makeup, has been doing it for ten years for forty-five minutes a day, and says she became addicted two months after she started. When she skips a day she feels unattractive and insecure, less capable of handling unusual situations. With it she has much more confidence.

Other people play musical instruments—the piano, the flute, the guitar, and the banjo are commonly mentioned—some sing, and many listen to music. These are all regarded by people as positively addicting. Practicing an instrument is perhaps more so for most than listening because it occupies one more and also provides more of a sense of accomplishment, but I suppose if one can become an addicted warm-bath taker, one can be an addicted listener. Although I have had no such responses, I would also venture that composing music must be for many a PA practice. Beethoven couldn't even hear his music much of his life but he heard it in his brain, and composing must to some extent have been a positive addiction that kept him going after he lost his hearing. Again, a word of caution. While any of these or similar activities can be pursued to addiction, it is my belief that this is extremely rare.

Yoga is both a physical and a mental discipline, and many people who practice yoga eventually reach PA. One woman reports that she stands in the bow position and vibrates in other positions taught to her in what she calls bioenergetics, which seems to be a type of yoga. Quite a few practice Hatha Yoga, which involves special physical exercises or asanas. Others stress yogic breathing or relaxation. But all these people are engaged in a rigorous physical and mental discipline which is either yoga or very close to it, whatever it may be called.

From here we go to the large group of physical addictions headed by running, but which also includes hiking, exercising, weight lifting, swimming, bicycling, and perhaps rock climbing or mountain climbing. Although rock climbing and mountain climbing are not something a person usually can do on a daily basis, I am sure the PA state which climbers occasionally reach in their activities is what motivates them. I don't believe that these can be classified in the same way as exercising or running but maybe they are to PA as a binge is to negative addiction. While running is the most common of all the physical positive addictions and will be discussed in detail in the next chapter, there are probably many more physical addictions than I have listed here. I make no claim to have discovered them all. Again, I stress that if an activity fulfills the six criteria stated earlier in this chapter it is potentially addicting. A friend of mine recently suggested that I should investigate bird watching as a potential PA activity. Considering the number of fanatic bird watchers, who is to say it's not?

Even though I have concluded that many respondents were not addicted, a careful study of their forms shows that there were a few addicts in almost all the previously described categories. Many reported the following experiences which are typical of PA. A man addicted to singing, who has been doing it for at least an hour a day for four years, says when he doesn't sing: "I feel lousy inside, lazy, like I haven't completed something. I am definitely a better musician but also a more confident person." Person after person describes the discomfort as feeling grumpy, hard to get along with, upset with himself or herself. Some say their day doesn't go right, and in most cases they say they feel guilt because they have missed something important that they didn't have to miss. In fact, many people just write the word "guilty" and that sums it up. Some people say they feel more tension, more nervousness, more self-doubt; others that they are more impatient, less communicative with others, and irritable. Several people describe fatigue, a feeling of tiredness or deadness, if they don't do their addicting thing. One person describes, "My mind feels a little muddled or foggy." All of these descriptions occur over and over again on the positive addiction form but they occur more in the physical addictions than in the mental practices.

Then we come to the question "What benefits do you receive from your addiction?" People, especially in the physical addictions or yoga, describe weight loss or an ability to control their weight where it was out of control before. Many say they have been able to give up bad habits, quite often excess drinking, sometimes smoking. People describe mental alertness, increased self-awareness, a physical feeling of well-being. Over and over again people report a *sense of confidence,* perhaps the single most often used words to describe the benefits of their addiction. Many describe that they are more tolerant and less angry. All of these are obviously tied to the increased mental strength discussed in the preceding chapter. All of the people who engage in the physical addictions—running, exercising—describe themselves in better physical shape naturally, but many of the people who engage in a purely mental addiction like meditation also describe physical benefits, especially an ability to control overweight. Both physical and mental positive addicts say they have more energy and need less sleep.

In the two chapters that follow I will discuss these benefits in much more detail. What is important here is to realize that PA is available to anyone. It has no age limits or activity limits. It can be attempted by the aged and the infirm, as well as by the young and the healthy. The only condition is that to get its benefits you have to do it usually for several months, sometimes for years.

Where you get the strength to do it long enough to gain more strength is a question I can't answer. It is like looking for your first job and being told only experienced people are hired. It's "Catch 22" except that people do get hired and people, even some weak people, do have the strength to become positively addicted. I believe that in the beginning the person is helped to continue by experiencing the non-self-critical state, which is pleasant and relaxing but not addicting. Later he may experience flashes of the PA state that further help to keep him going. While all positive addicts must do something they want to do, what is most important, I believe, is to figure out how to do whatever it is that you choose in such a way that you can accept yourself completely and noncritically as you do it. If you can't do this, then you have little chance to become addicted. So, if you choose, choose carefully. Don't expect too much of yourself and don't make a big deal about the fact that you are attempting to become addicted. Go quietly. It's a personal thing. Keep it that way and you have a good chance to reach PA.

five

RUNNING—THE HARDEST BUT SUREST WAY TO POSITIVE ADDICTION

You would be wrong to emphasize the pain. I think the mind doesn't recall pain, pain is anesthetized by the euphoria of running . . . you are going to get blisters. They were very bad in the last six months at Harlow but I stopped paying attention to them so they just stopped handing out signals. There is a part of every marathon where something does take over . . . a sensation of movement. E. M. Forster wrote a story about rowers in which he said they reached a state of transcendentalism which was the goal of every sportsman. You lose a sense of identity in yourself, you become running itself. I get this in training. I only have to think of putting on my running shoes and the kinesthetic pleasure of floating along, the pleasure of movement starts to come. I get a feeling of euphoria, almost real happiness. It's an unvicious circle; when I am happy I am running well and when I am running well I am happy. . . . It is the platonic idea of knowing thyself. Running is getting to know yourself to an extreme degree.

This quote from Ian Thompson,* a world champion marathon runner, explains why many runners are addicted. The

*London Sunday *Times* (June 30, 1974).

loss of the sense of yourself, the floating, the euphoria, the statement "you become running itself," are classic descriptions of the PA state.

In the October 1974 issue of *Runner's World*, Joe Henderson, the editor, published my questionnaire titled "Help Wanted." Henderson was very interested in my concept of running as a positive addiction and describes himself as an eighteen-year running addict.

HELP WANTED

Dr. William Glasser, a Los Angeles psychiatrist best known for his book *Reality Therapy,* is working out a new theory that involves runners and other athletes. He wants help from all the runners he can reach.

"I am collecting data on a large number of people who engage in some voluntary self-improvement activity," says Dr. Glasser, "to test what I believe is a fascinating psychological hypothesis."

He doesn't want to spell out exactly what the hypothesis is "because it would prejudice the data. But I promise to report on my findings in a future magazine."

Fill out the information below (on a separate sheet) and return your questionnaire to *Runner's World,* Box 366, Mountain View, Calif. 94040, for forwarding to Dr. Glasser. Letters addressed to him will be sent along unopened to insure confidentiality. The doctor adds, "I would appreciate it very much if you would include your name, address, age and occupation, as I may wish to contact you directly for more data."

1. How long have you been running regularly?
2. How many days a week do you run?
3. How many hours a day?
4. Do you run competitively?
5. If yes, would you still run if you didn't compete?

6. Do you strive for some improvement—even a small bit?

7. Do you run alone?

8. If you run with others, would you still run if you had to run alone?

9. How many scheduled runs in the last six months have you skipped?

10. If the previous number is over 20, what is the main reason you missed?

11. Do you (always) (mostly) (sometimes) (rarely) (never) enjoy your day's run?

12. Are you uncomfortable if you miss your day's run?

13. If you are uncomfortable, will you describe the discomfort you experience?

14. How many months were you running before you began to experience the previously described discomfort?

15. Can you relieve the discomfort in any way besides running?

16. If yes, how?

17. What direct physical benefits have you received from running? (If the next two questions don't make sense to you, skip them.)

18. Can you describe the main state of your mind when you are settled into your day's run?

19. Can you achieve this previously described state of mind in any other way? If yes, how?

20. Since you became a runner, have you been able to overcome any bad habits or personal disabilities which you couldn't overcome before (smoking, drinking, gambling, overeating, shyness, lateness, etc.)? Please describe, and if the change is major, give details.

21. Do you have any other self-imposed task on a regular basis, like meditation, yoga, practicing a musical instrument, etc.?

22. Would you recommend running to an interested non-runner?

It was not possible to place the questionnaire all on the same page of the magazine, so I thought I would get only a limited response. I was not prepared for the avalanche that descended upon me—almost seven hundred replies from a subscription list of twenty thousand. As I suspected, about 75 percent of the runners who responded and who have been running regularly for a year, at least six days a week for an hour, are addicted. The two key questions, "Do you suffer if you miss a run?" and "Do you always enjoy your run?" are both answered with an emphatic yes. While many race, they would almost all run whether they competed or not; in fact, many did not really enjoy running until they stopped competing. They almost all run for an hour a day, most run six days a week, many seven, a few five. Quite a few who run alone six days a week run in a social group on Sundays.

When they tell of their discomfort, what they describe is very similar to the classic withdrawal symptoms of a negative addiction. Joe Henderson, who had to lay off once for almost a month when he had a foot operation, describes his discomfort as apathy, sluggishness, weight loss due to no appetite, sleeplessness, headaches, and stomach aches. He says, "I just lost something I'd come to crave."

The addiction to running does not come quickly. It rarely happens until the runner has built enough endurance so that he can run effortlessly for an hour. For most this takes at least six months, for many longer. Joe Henderson, who has been running for eighteen years, took two years to become addicted. It happens faster in older runners who didn't start with school competition, but until any runner becomes addicted he must run on the faith that what he is doing is good for him physically, which, of course, it is. Once addicted, runners will run for as long as they can—those in their seventies and eighties are not uncommon.

When they are forced through illness or injury to stop

running, some runners can reduce their withdrawal pain through exercises, others through meditation. Joe Henderson took up bike riding, which helped, but it wasn't as good as running. He says that there is nothing like the feel of your feet against the road, the pleasure of motion produced by your own body. Almost all runners emphasize the pleasure of motion, the gliding or floating that Ian Thompson describes in the opening paragraph. I believe that running creates the optimal condition for PA because it is our most ancient and still most effective survival mechanism. We are descended from those who ran to stay alive, and this need to run is programmed genetically into our brains. When we have gained the endurance to run long distances easily, then a good run reactivates the ancient neural program. As this occurs we reach a state of mental preparedness that leads to a basic feeling of satisfaction *that is less self-critical than any other activity that we can do alone.*

If you wish confirmation of the genetic need to run, watch a child. You will see that it is almost as if the child has consciously to learn to walk but not to run. See the parents of a two- or three-year-old constantly nagging at their child to slow down, to stop running. Urged to run by a neural program written millions of years ago, the child, like a puppy, runs naturally. He has no choice but to try to develop this activity, which he needs much less for survival than his ancient ancestors but he still needs it. It is hard to survive childhood if you can't run. It is only in very recent times that most adults haven't had to run for survival, and if you live near the center of one of our large cities, you might well take issue with this statement.

It is because this activity is so non-self-critical and so completely programmed in the ancient pathways of our brains that when we run without fatigue we are able to free most of the brain for other activity. When this happens it is easy to slip into the euphoric, unique PA state. While I am sure this state was valuable to primitive man when he ran easily during times of no stress, it seems even more important today. Many anthropologists believe our brains are poorly equipped to cope with the stresses produced by civilization. Simply stated, we need more neural pathways than most of us have, and if we can get these through running we would be foolish not to consider this possibility, especially if we are finding it difficult to cope with any aspect of our lives.

To run for strength means to run for addiction. It is the PA state that is so valuable. The responses to my questionnaire indicate that many runners reach it. They don't describe it the same way, although there are similarities. Some can't describe it at all, which makes sense, because when our minds are totally spun out there is no tangible experience to describe. What the respondents tell about is the feeling that accompanies this occurrence. Sometimes there is an occasional conscious realization when a thinking or experiencing pathway is activated but often there is consciously little more than what Ian Thompson said: "Where something does take over, not just you, but a sensation of movement." Like Thompson, few people can describe the something that takes over, but they experience the feeling that something has. It is this feeling, usually very pleasurable, often euphoric, that is the core of the PA experience.

In the following excerpts from responses to my questionnaire I try to bring you the flavor of this experience. Some runners are much more articulate than others, some have experienced the PA state much more than others. It does not follow that because you can't describe it you experience it less or more. There is no guarantee that if you run you will experience any of the following sensations or thoughts, but what you experience may be as valuable for you as these respondents claim their feeling has been for them. What I can say is that if you are willing to put in the time to become addicted to running, there will be a payoff in increased strength. But you have to make the effort, perhaps up to two years of effort, so while running is perhaps the surest way, it is not the easiest way to the PA state.

Martha Clopfer, a thirty-nine-year-old farmwife and part-time teacher, has for five years been running six or seven times a week, a half-hour to three hours a day. Sometimes she runs alone and sometimes she runs with her husband. She enjoys running and takes a day off only when she feels a cold coming on. She says, "If I miss running several days in a row a physical sluggishness sets in, including constipation and a mental sluggishness to match." It took her about a year until this kind of discomfort came on a regular basis, but Martha doesn't suffer much because she has missed only five runs in the last six months. She describes some physical benefits as "fewer and milder colds, weight control while eating everything I want, a little lower heart rate," but in answer to question 18, which asks her state of mind when she runs, she says:

> Meditative is probably the best single word but it is a different state from Quaker meeting type meditation. The most similar state of mind I know comes when listening to music for pleasure. The rhythm of running is a strong element. Sometimes problems get solved while I am running or I think of things to say to people but it is not a figuring out process. More of a sudden flash of insight that comes when you are least trying to find an answer. I think worrying and running are impossible to do at the same time.

I quote Martha's answer because many other people have answered question 18 in a similar way. The brain takes care of things on its own when it is given a chance, and in the PA state it may unconsciously solve problems—the only conscious evidence that it has done so being the flash of insight that many addicted runners describe. In this state everything is floating around in your mind, including your problems, and at times a solution pops into your mind without effort, almost like a spinning roulette ball falling on the right number.

Timothy Charles Masters is twenty-four and has been running for four years. He runs four times a week, fifteen miles each time, about an hour and forty-five minutes a day. He runs competitively but would still run if he didn't compete. He runs alone. In the last six months he has missed no scheduled runs. He emphasizes the "no" by putting a "none" after it. He enjoys his day's running and he is uncomfortable if he misses. He describes the discomfort: "When I miss my workouts I feel as though I have let myself down. My personal integrity suffers a blow. Guilt feelings mount continuously until I run again." But as he has missed none in the last six months this suffering is now academic. He goes on to say, "I am glad, however, that I feel this way because it is the watchdog which makes sure I do my running. Contrary to what this freedom and rights oriented society says or thinks, I have to run." He says that the discomfort at missing a run came gradually but began to be apparent after two to three months as he got into longer runs. He claims that he cannot relieve this discomfort by any method he has tried. Leg stretches and sit-ups give some relief and he tries to tell himself that it really doesn't matter that much to skip a day. He tells himself, "Your shins could stand a day off, you really have been running hard the past few weeks." However, this doesn't in any way relieve the pain of the missed workouts. It just buys a little time. He says his heart rate is down to 46, his weight is 150 for a 5-foot-10 height, he doesn't have to worry about eating, and he describes that he is in the best cardiovascular condition possible. This knowledge that he is in good shape, he says, "gives me all the self-confidence I will ever need."

He further describes that "running has also changed my outlook on life, material things aren't important anymore. Besides my family responsibilities I can't think of anything more vitally important to myself than a good hard 15-mile run or a sub-three hour marathon."

In answer to question 18 on his mental state he says:

When I am settled into my run I concentrate on running as much as possible but the mind wanders to thoughts of most anything. The state of mind is one of almost total complacency and privacy. Although you are in sight of people, cars, buses, school kids, dogs, etc., I feel a very privateness when I run. People may yell at me or a kid may bug me for a few hundred yards but due to the nature of running (it is hard and physically demanding) you are pretty much left to yourself and no one can invade your runner's world because they physically are not able. If another runner enters or intrudes it is fine because he is running for the same reasons and for a lot of the same feelings.

As for recommending running (and again this is thoughtful and worth recording), he says:

I would definitely recommend running to a non-runner but not on the crusader level. Whenever I am in circles where talk runs to physical fitness I always sling my barbs of sarcasm and I will make suggestions of running but I won't crusade if anyone asks me about running. I am completely open to their questions and try to encourage—not crusade.

He finishes with a voluntary statement:

Running is extremely personal to each runner, its importance shapes the lives of many people who enjoy running long distances. I can really never see myself quitting unless an accident should occur. It has been an integral part of my life for a number of years and I am quite happy with myself and my life and I wouldn't trade places with anyone.

John Roemer, III, fills out my questionnaire in some detail but also includes this note: "While I am not generally enamored of psychological studies, I am afflicted with runner's mouth and the proclivity of runners to jabber about running in general and their own training in particular." He then goes on to say that at thirty-six he has been running for about five and a half years, six times a week. He runs for one hour and forty-five minutes a day when he is in marathon training, one hour and fifteen minutes a day when he is not. He races but he would run even if he didn't compete. In his words, "Competition is the spice, running the main course." In the last six months he has skipped five runs, three due to injury, one travel day and one tired day. He enjoys his run unless he is struggling with a serious injury.

In answer to question 12 he says, "If I miss a day's run it is not just uncomfortable, it is a disaster," then goes on to say what the disaster is:

> It's a loss of a pleasurable activity, inability to take a crap, fidgety anger at whatever caused me to miss the run or whatever is handy, guilt—good runners probably run on sore tendons—extraordinary depression, literally feeling that life is pointless.

It is terrible if he is forced by injury to take a long layoff—he had two in five and a half years, four and a half weeks from sore knees from a fifty-mile race in 1973, three weeks from a sore tendon in January 1974—"The latter was like facing the grave because I thought my running career might be over." His discomfort from not running started, he suspects, very shortly but was certainly present after six months.

As to what will relieve the agony of not running (question 15) John says:

> There is nothing that will relieve the agony of not running. Walking, biking, swimming and sex are pleasant enough. I have speculated that one or two of them might be a substitute if I permanently ruptured a tendon, but walking, biking, or swimming are to running as masturbation is to making love, a bit better than abstinence.

He describes a lot of good physical benefits and then describes his state of mind: "I enjoy physical and mental satisfaction, feeling that everything is all right, elimination of worries." He agrees with Martha Clopfer, who said running and worrying don't mix. John Roemer goes on to say, "I can't carry a personal or job problem all the way through a run. They fade into inconsequence, thoughts become long, slow motion, drawn out. I often kick my mind out of gear." He experiences "heightened awareness of light, temperature, and odors, sometimes an inexpressible joy. I want to stick my arms out and float." If you could read all the questionnaires you would see that statement made over and over again: I want to fly or float. One person said, "It is as if my mind is floating along beside my body looking at it in a kind of humorous way, watching it struggle to run while it (the mind) is free-floating along, ahead of it, behind it, below it, above it." In answer to question 19 Roemer talks about swimming and says a long swim comes closest to replacing a run. It probably would have been helpful if I could have investigated swimmers for this book because I am sure that the PA state occurs in swimming, but as I said, man ran for survival, he did not swim for survival. Swimming, therefore, is learned; it is not a natural survival activity and is not programmed in our brains. Interestingly enough, of all the questionnaires I got back only one person was an addicted swimmer. She had originally been a runner, had hurt herself and gone into swimming because she couldn't run, and found it almost to be as satisfactory.

In terms of psychological benefit, John says:

> I have never had any seriously bad habits but running has been responsible for reducing frenetic nervous drive, compulsive overwork, and impatient demand for immediate social change. I am much less serious, far more easygoing, less committed to abolishing all the evils overnight, easier to live with, have greater ability to ignore and eschew peripheral issues and that jazz.

And he says while he used to hold forth on all issues at all meetings, now "frequently I am silent and unless I have something substantial and unique to offer I don't say anything." He claims to be more joyful, more ready to flow with being and, as I said, he doesn't really have any other self-imposed tasks besides running. In answer to question 22, about recommending running to others, he says:

> Everybody should run. It would drown hates, aggression, make people happier, create a greater sense of self-worth. I have speculated about using regular running with occasional competition for prisons, mental patients, kids in school. If everybody ran, the revolution would be accomplished, the automobile eliminated, idiotic luxuries and compulsions abolished, proper priorities established, the environment saved, classes of racism ended.

Here it is interesting to note that what he claims from running is almost exactly what the Maharishi Mahesh Yogi claims would happen if everybody practiced transcendental meditation. Will positive addiction save the world? I doubt it, but I am sure more of it would help. John Roemer goes on to say:

> Most folks who take a stab at running drop out. They may try too much at once or they run in awful places [he runs in the woods] or they don't like the little pain or they can't get up in the morning. To run you have got to build yourself up around a half-hour, hour, whatever, in which you run and say that absolutely nothing else is to interfere with this.

Here he mentions something noted by many runners, that it is best to run in a peaceful natural place. The more one has to attend to distractions the more difficult it is to enjoy the run. Barking dogs who chase seem to be the bane of all runners.

Jim Corey is twenty-seven years old and has been running for eleven years, five days a week, an hour a day. He has run competitively for eight of the last eleven years but for the last three years has been doing mostly what he describes as "fun running." He has an interesting comment which bears out my contention that the necessary condition for positive addiction is the non-self-critical state. In question 13 he describes his discomfort, as most runners do, revolving around feelings of guilt and self-disdain for being lazy, coupled with the feeling of loss for missing a pleasurable experience. But then in question 14, where I ask how long it took before the person began to get this discomfort regularly, Corey says:

> In my new role as a non-competitor and a fun runner, I experienced the discomfort within one or two months. As a competitor in high school and college where I was

expected to run I experienced no discomfort about missing a day's run but rather something akin to the feeling of a hooky player's relief at getting out of a boring grinding task.

This again bears out the fact that it is something that you have to want to do, and at which you cannot lose. If someone chased you with a gun and tried to get you positively addicted to running I don't think he would be any more successful than if he chased you with a gun and tried to get you negatively addicted to heroin. Jim describes his mental state:

I can describe two states of mind when I have settled into my runs. Sometimes both will occur during the course of a run, sometimes only one will occur when I am settled into a run. Strangely enough these minds seem to be a function of the weather. Nice crisp days yeah, hot humid days, boo. Novelty of the course, physical features of the course include whether the course is beautiful, easy to run on, etc. The first mind state that I would describe is that of a rational cognitive nature and coincides with runs that are generally unsatisfactory in some way. The weather is hot, the dogs are harassing me, the course is becoming boring because I have been on it many times. The second mind state is [and here I believe he describes the PA state quite clearly] not cognitive or rational, instead it is ego-transcending. I simply perceive as I run. I react instinctively to obstacles which suddenly appear. I float. I run like a deer. I feel good. I feel high. I don't think at all. My awareness is only of the present. Even that cannot be called awareness. Brain chatter is gone. This mind set normally coincides with running alone on a cross-country course in autumn on a crisp day but definitely appears other times of the year as well.

He says in answer to question 20:

I am a less uptight person since rediscovering running.
I believe I have seen goodness by virtue of my runs. This
awareness of the goodness in the world allows me to
see it in people. I am more open with people and it
seems to make them more open to me, thus my inter-
personal habits or skills have improved.

Matt Brown, a physician, age forty-eight, answers my questionnaire:

As a physician I think I have more insight into what
these benefits may be than the average person. I would
have been more flip on this a couple of years ago with
all the right answers. I don't worry much about my
health and never did; I have come up with no injuries
other than a rare blister. I did well on a stress test in July
(that would be a cardiovascular test) but I find the whole
procedure quite boring [talking about how healthy running is] from the subject's point of view. I have no illu-
sions that I have found a way to halt the aging process
but I also sense a certain envy on the part of friends and
acquaintances.

What Matt Brown is saying is that a lot of runners
who develop a greatly lowered pulse rate and blood
pressure may get the delusion that they are not going
to get old. I think he says it quite clearly: "You will be
in better shape but even if you run you are going to get
old." In answer to question 18, the main state of your
mind when you are settled into your run, he says:

This sounds like the nitty gritty. Sometimes and always
at first it feels like a comfortable ritual, like a classroom
routine for a student or tuning your fiddle or scrubbing
before surgery. From this you can go into conversation
with a companion for slow miles, you are concentrating
on keeping up if it is a fast workout and all kinds of
extraneous things can enter. Daydreaming is possible
but I find that prolonged reverie is as difficult as prolonged logical thinking while running. A thought might

occur which sounds as good as a line of poetry but it is very hard to develop this for more than two or three lines. Often during the run a self-centered state develops in which you feel yourself as a total organism working very hard, a high state of function which is generally a good feeling and overrides minor discomfort such as blisters. I doubt if this is mystical, only animal. I am not entirely sure of the difference. One is conscious of the environment in different ways. At different times I am sure it can meld into the inner state.

I think he confirms my contention that this is an ancient survival state of mind which, as he describes in his last sentence, "melds" into the PA state.

A thoughtful thirty-eight-year-old businessman, Ronald Rombalski, has an answer to question 18 concerning his state of mind which I think gives a further insight into the PA state. He says:

> If I am tired the first mile of any run is difficult because my mind is driving my body to run. After the first mile my subconscious takes over and my body functions automatically. My mind is then free to wander and does. Only when I run hard for a short distance, run hard uphill, or run very long distances is my mind functioning with respect to running and actually driving my body. I cannot categorize my thoughts while running and I have attempted to do so over the past two or three years. All I can say is that my mind is not on my body, or on my immediate surroundings. It is as though my mind is resting in a vacuum. Please note I use the word resting not the word functioning.

Then he says something that many other running addicts agree on: "In fact, running has imparted a feeling of superiority over those who do not run." It is not a feeling of egocentric superiority, it is just a feeling that there is something about most runners that makes them feel a little better than other people. It has to do with the fact that they think they have a better life because they run.

Richard Carr, a forty-year-old man who runs four to five times a week and states he has recorded 5,244 miles since August 17, 1969, when he started. He says if he doesn't run his brain seems to get cluttered and he also stresses that he has to get out to run. He says he ran in place in the bathroom one winter and besides messing up the house plumbing, didn't do much but keep from losing all he gained. He lists a lot of benefits from running but when he talks about his mental state he says:

> A sense of specialness, victory, cleanliness, timeless-ness, friendliness, a sort of positive loneliness, a kind of a long stretched out masturbation, only with a shin-ing infinite future involving the whole mind and body and all surroundings, past, present and forever. There must be something religious there too, because it all seems so right with eternity, personally and collec-tively.

His psychological benefits were such that:

> Shyness and staying up late were conquered early without realizing it, and now my capacity has in-creased in all directions and the only things I don't do more of now are watch TV, drink and waste time in general. Although I relax much better in social situa-tions and can enjoy just sitting and talking much bet-ter than before."

The next statement from William Bat tends to verify my belief that whatever the positive addiction state is it can be achieved in several different ways but it, the state, is con-stant. In answer to question 18, what is your mental state:

I think it can best be described as a state of sublimation similar to that experienced during transcendental meditation. For me it is a period free from mental stress and structured thought, a time for me to lose myself in nature. Several times I have begun my run with the intention of thinking out a problem but this doesn't seem to work for me. I immediately get caught up in the pure and simple act of running.

When asked if he can achieve it any other way he further confirms this by saying: "By practicing transcendental meditation, but this requires two twenty-minute periods daily and relative privacy, neither of which is easy to find in today's typical lifestyle."

Although I have mentioned as a benefit of PA that people are able to give up bad habits like smoking, I think that William Bat expresses it well when he says, "I began smoking at age fifteen and when I quit twenty months ago, I had advanced to two to three packs per day [he has been running about two years]." I think running is as incompatible with smoking as it is with worrying; in fact, since worrying and smoking go so well together an increase in strength seems to eliminate both for most runners.

Betsy White, who is thirty-six and the mother of three children, has been running for two years, every day for an hour. She is already addicted and feels fat, lazy, generally slothful, and grouchy when she doesn't run, feelings which occurred two to three months after she started. She feels physically stronger but it is her mental state that she describes in some detail in a questionnaire that otherwise is comprised mostly of short answers. She responds to question 18:

It varies. Sometimes my mind is very active planning other things such as menus, scheduling family activities or whatever research or writing I am currently involved in. Other times my mind sort of empties itself, making me intensely aware of the surrounding scene and the rhythm of my breathing and motion. The second state of mind is more relaxing but I sometimes have accomplished a lot when in the first state of mind, composed several pages' worth of writing or other work.

Here Betsy differs from some of the others who say they can't really do this. I think the others are more into PA and she, as I will discuss in the next chapter, is more into the pre-PA state. Here, because she is non-self-critical, her brain is more accessible, but she is not spun out in what she describes as her first state.

Phillip Simon, who is thirty-five years of age, has been running for four years. Like most runners he says, "I am frustrated, aggravated, hostile, irritable, and generally unpleasant when I miss a day's run," but in the past six months this addicted runner hasn't missed a day. In answer to question 14 he, like several others, has written something I think again clearly states the slowly addicting nature of running:

The time didn't seem as important as the commitment. At first I only intended to run a couple of days a week and if I ran one day instead of another it didn't seem to matter. After I decided to run more often and also farther, I began to feel that I couldn't miss a day I intended to run. In more specific response to your question, I think that about eight months after I began running I felt I could not miss.

And now he runs every day.

I include his answer to question 18 because he says:

I never come home from a run mad unless someone has almost run over me or something like that but I am not upset enough to affect the run. As a matter of fact, like last night, when I had a close call, I was far enough from home that I lapsed back into my thought process before I reached home.

In talking about his close call he confirms the Toronto runner's claim that running in the PA state can be dangerous, and when he states he never comes home from a run mad he supports the statements of many of my respondents that running is also incompatible with anger. I believe anger is our most self-critical experience and, as I have said already, running may be our most accepting. To question 20, Phillip answers:

Let me give a little background before answering the points directly. Four years ago spring I weighed about 100 pounds more than I do now, 250. I was active and played handball several times a week and didn't feel all that out of shape. I had smoked since early teenhood and had stopped just prior to putting on about 65 pounds. I drank and ate with little care of the results.

He then adds:

To make a long story short, I no longer drink anything alcoholic and don't smoke, and watch my diet very closely. I think that these changes are directly related to my running program. I don't object to drink for others—my wife both smokes and drinks. We serve guests in our home and I still maintain a rather good selection at the bar. I don't feel smoking and drinking are consistent with serious running and if I ever stopped [running], which I do not intend to do, I may even take an occasional drink.

Then at the end of his questionnaire he says:

Yesterday I ran after I had read the article and had begun to answer the questionnaire. I tried to think about what I think about when I run because it seems different sitting at this machine [typewriter] than it does out along the road. I found myself going for long stretches without really thinking about anything in particular. I seem to run along and watch the places where I would be stepping but not for any reason. I tried once to run with a portable radio and an earphone; it was not satisfactory. I felt the radio interfered or invaded my privacy. I have not used it again even though it was not burdensome or uncomfortable in any way as a physical problem.

Simon states clearly one of the important features of the PA state, the sense of satisfactory privacy, the temporary abolition of the need for others as one enjoys the run.

John Read, a businessman, describes his state of mind when he is running:

Sometimes I am able to concentrate and solve a difficult problem that has been bothering me for days or longer. Other times I engage in a kind of conscious euphoria and enjoy it to the hilt, knowing full well that I don't have the accompanying feelings of guilt that I used to have often after becoming high on alcohol.

He describes his past life as being that of an almost hopeless alcoholic. Then he says, in answer to the question on the psychological benefits he has gotten from his running:

I am always energetic and enthusiastic, I think quicker and clearer, I always feel like I always wanted to feel by having a few drinks. I successfully quit drinking before I began serious running but running has completely destroyed any desire to drink. Even if someone could prove to me that I could now safely engage in moderate social drinking I would have absolutely no desire to do so. I am perfectly relaxed and can enjoy myself completely at a cocktail party sipping my ginger ale on the rocks.

To say that is a very satisfying feeling would be a gross understatement as evidenced by the following note Read added to the bottom of the questionnaire:

I am a forty-eight-year-old businessman writing this on a plane during a business trip. Running has brought about a fantastically wonderful change in my life that assures me of never having to return to a way of life that came very close to destroying me.

Here again, we are beginning to see the power that a positive addiction has in helping a person to overcome a negative addiction. Certainly I can't recommend that positive addiction is the cure-all for negative addiction. I don't think there is any "cure-all" for weakness, but I do believe that it is an avenue that hasn't been sufficiently explored. Possibly, people who have the energy to pursue a negative addiction, *because it is something that they can do on their own and not depend on others for its satisfaction, could pursue a positive addiction for the same reason.* They may not have the strength to go out and find love and worth, which for them are chancy, but they might have the strength to pursue running, which doesn't require others. If they could, there is a possibility that they could get the same benefits that John Read so eloquently describes.

Gordy Shafer, thirty-nine years old, a dentist, has lost his excess weight and has completely eliminated a chronic low-back problem. He says he no longer needs as much sleep, as he experiences the usual cardiovascular changes for the better. His answer to number 18 is:

Probably I could write a book on that subject. Generally I could best describe the feeling as a sense of confidence, of well-being coupled with an absolute sense of withdrawal from the rest of the world. For a while the world completely stops while I am engaged in my run. This does not happen in competition. There, there is a sharp concentration and alertness, almost the opposite of the daily run.

Again, we can see the negative effect of competition on the passively pleasurable PA state, but this is balanced by the active pleasure of competition. Many runners combine the two successfully but, as Shafer says, they are very different experiences. He continues:

The closest feelings I can compare it to are those occasions when a person is in the very beginning stages of intoxication with alcohol. The so-called happy or warm feeling or glow. After a run I have a great feeling of satisfaction and readiness for any challenge, sort of a superego just the opposite of competition. Post race there is usually a feeling that I could have done better, why didn't I, I will do better the next time, often a mixture of failure and satisfaction. Even after a personal best I feel I should have performed better. I can't achieve the nonracing feeling entirely or completely *in any other manner.* The closest might be with the use of alcohol, as far as sense of well-being and no interference from the outside world goes. I think what I mean is a sense of euphoria, the closest state of mind to sex, as far as the sense of absolute withdrawal from the rest of the world goes. Heck, no wonder I like to run every day. Who wouldn't enjoy a daily diet of a drunken orgy? I guess I have just formed my own hypothesis while at the typewriter.

There is little to add to these descriptions. Running, perhaps because it is our most basic solitary survival activity, produces the non-self-critical state more effectively than any other practice. If it were up to me to suggest a positive addiction for anyone no matter what his present state of strength, from the weakest addict to the strongest among us, I would suggest running. By starting slowly and carefully, getting checked by a physician if there is any question of health, and working up to the point where one can run an hour without fatigue, it is almost certain that the PA state will be achieved on a fairly regular basis. How long this takes depends upon the person, but if there is no attempt at competition and the runner runs alone in a pleasant natural setting, addiction should occur within a year. Joe Henderson says running isn't for everyone, but it seems obvious to me that it would be unbelievably good for a lot more of us than run now.

six

MEDITATION—THE MOST POPULAR WAY TO POSITIVE ADDICTION

Although many practices of meditation have been proved valuable for centuries and still are, the general public was little aware of them until about fifteen years ago when the Maharishi Mahesh Yogi came upon the scene with his concept of Transcendental Meditation, or TM. I think of the Maharishi as the Henry Ford of meditation and I say this in admiration. He has taken a concept that, in terms of reaching the masses, lay dormant for thousands of years and made it a valuable part of the daily life of over half a million people, with thousands more beginning each month. One of the Maharishi's great contributions is his ability to remove much of the false mystery and most of the intellectual snobbery and religiosity from meditation. TM has made the practice easily accessible to everyone. The Maharishi is an acute businessman who has commercially exploited these contributions into a worldwide organization which energetically pushes the benefits of his teaching. There are those who fault him for these accomplishments but judging by the numbers of dedicated followers, many of whom work for little or no pay, I would have to conclude that TM has grown because it has value. It is beneficial even if the practitioner does not reach the PA state, as I will explain shortly. But from the standpoint of this book its greatest value is that it is a simple, easy-to-learn mantra meditation* through which many people are able to reach the PA state regularly. If this occurs they are positively addicted, with all the previously described benefits.

In this chapter I will not try to teach the concepts of TM or of any other equally valuable meditation, any more than I would attempt to teach you how to run. If you want to learn meditation, there are plenty of qualified teachers. It is evident, however, that many people have enjoyed both the meditation experience and the positive effect this process has had upon their lives. They are continuing to meditate and they are also trying in unprecedented numbers to convince their friends to try it. The following quote from Cynthia Powell, a twenty-four-year-old South Carolina schoolteacher, speaks eloquently to this point:

> I have filled out your questionnaire but as I read over it I don't seem to have said what I think about meditation. . . . I want everyone to start meditating. It has been the biggest change in my life, I think really ever. I can't understand why it works, . . . but I know that it does work, that is, it changes people. It has changed me and I wasn't even out to be changed. I thought I was just fine the way I was. I just began meditating because my husband was going to start and families get a cheaper fee. Also as I said on the questionnaire, I felt that any experience would be beneficial and I was looking forward to meeting some of the "weird" people who do this sort of thing. (Now I am one of them. I surely like being weird better than I liked being normal) . . . I went into this experience with *absolutely no* expectations and now I cannot count the things that have changed

*TM is a meditation technique that employs a mantra, a specific sound or a Sanskrit word that is claimed to be tailored to the student by his teacher to use as an essential part of his meditation.

about my life and I feel that the reason has to be meditation. Don't you want to hear some of these changes? Sure you do! (I am still a little insecure and feel foolish about this letter.) In the first place I lost about eighteen pounds. I never thought I was fat before but now I feel so much better and I don't eat nervously all the time as I used to. When I began meditating this summer I was working on my Master's Degree. I had always thought school was sort of a drag before. I was just going to graduate from school because it raised my salary but this summer I began to really *love to study.* I began to go to my professors' offices and ask them questions. I did all of my assignments and more just because I was so interested in the courses that I was taking. This is the fourth year of my teaching school and it is certainly my best year. I never seem to tire of giving my students of myself, they in turn will do almost anything for me. I just feel that I see things more clearly. Always before I thought of my class as a whole class, now I think of it as individuals and it all makes teaching so much easier and so much more fun. Socially I have had much closer relationships with my friends and it is easier for me to get to know people. I feel confident in myself; I feel I have something worthwhile to say. Also my plants grow better. I remember now to water them. I can think of about a dozen more changes I have had. As I am writing this letter I am thinking about not sending it to you, but heck, if more meditators were more verbal about their experiences then maybe more people would begin meditating and then we wouldn't feel so competitive and insecure and suspicious.

In my effort to get a simple questionnaire filled out by meditators like Mrs. Powell, I approached the TM organization because it not only has access to large numbers of meditators, it also supports research on TM. Unfortunately, the TM people did not cooperate, for two reasons. They objected to my asking what goes on in the meditator's head and also to calling meditation an addiction. They were against my asking what goes on in a meditator's head, claiming this is unimportant and conclusions should not be drawn from it. What's really important, the TM people maintain, is what does not go on in his head. I agree in principle but for the purposes of research this principle must be occasionally compromised, because it is a fact that things do go on in meditators' heads while they successfully meditate and what goes on is of interest to this study. As this chapter continues you will see that many meditators, most of whom practice TM, were able to report their experiences in a way which I believe adds to the knowledge in the field. TM people should have more faith in both its effectiveness and in the strength of those who practice it. None of the respondents was hurt by *briefly introspecting on one occasion* about what went through his mind during a typical meditation. The meditators were both able and willing to describe quite clearly the PA state that many reached occasionally and a few reached regularly as they meditated. The TM people were also upset that I called meditation a positive addiction, and after studying about seven hundred questionnaires I would partly agree with them. Meditators who reach the PA state with any frequency do become addicted, but many do not reach this state or reach it so seldom it is not addicting. They continue the practice, however, and I think it is important that I explain why meditation or any other mental practice described in Chapter Four is beneficial even if the PA state is never or seldom reached.

Most of the seven hundred runners who responded to my runners' questionnaire reached the highly pleasurable PA state frequently. Because they do, almost all runners suffer from moderate to very severe withdrawal when they miss several runs. Meditators suffer much less. Fewer than 40 percent mention any kind of discomfort at all, fewer than 5 percent could be described as suffering a great deal when they miss. This doesn't mean meditation isn't beneficial but it does not provide as frequent access to the PA state, and its benefits are accordingly less. What meditation does for all meditators is to provide a regular time each day to accept what goes on in one's head in a non-self-critical way. In doing so the meditator quickly gains more access to his brain, an access not usually achieved by most of us who never take this regular time off to be non-self-critical. As this occurs there is a marked physical relaxation because any access to the mental strength we have is immediately reflected in physical relaxation. For some this is as far as they get; they never are able to go farther into the highly pleasurable, intensely personal, noncognitive PA-state experience. Why they can't I am not sure, but I believe they are rarely able to leave their minds sufficiently alone. Therefore, they find it impossible to get out of their heads as frequently as do the runners when they are into a run, when their brains become almost totally superfluous to their activity. However, as I will discuss later in this chapter, at least 80 percent of those who follow the instruction of their teachers carefully do succeed in experiencing flashes of the PA state on a fairly regular basis. On the other hand, there *are* a few who manage to achieve it regularly enough to become positively addicted, but they are unable to report how. Probably, as they get the brief flashes that most meditators experience, they learn to accept these occurrences completely with no attempt at introspection. The flashes become longer and tend to come more frequently, and if they occur often enough the meditators may become addicted. It may never be learned exactly how they do it; we certainly don't know now.

In terms of PA, however, the common, pleasant, relaxing, but nonaddicting meditation experience (usually with brief flashes of PA) is valuable because it happens quickly, sometimes after the first time. This makes it fairly easy to keep going, much easier than running, so in the end, although it is a much less sure way to reach the PA state, meditation probably does make the PA state available to more people than any other practice. It is interesting to read the responses of many meditators which clearly indicate frequent but brief PA experiences. They often report a fleeting but pleasant headache, which I think is a flash of the expanding PA state. They report it with surprise, as if it were not supposed to occur, and they are equally surprised when the headache is pleasant. Cynthia Powell, who previously described meditation in such glowing terms but who has been meditating only six months, tells of a slightly different experience: "Sometimes I see something like black and white circles coming and going but it is very rare." Most of the time she describes the typical, relaxed, non-self-critical flow of ideas which come and go effortlessly but which are much different from these flashes. Perhaps this is as close as she will ever get to the PA state, yet no one will deny she has already gotten much strength from what she does. I believe, however, that if she continues for another six months to a year, she will go further into PA and she may arrive at her equivalent of where Mary Kay Corcoran, a thirty-three-year-old nursery schoolteacher and a one-year meditator, seems to be. Mary Kay reports:

> I used to feel myself sort of going into my head deeper and deeper. Now I am not aware of this but sometimes I am more aware of recent dreams during part of the meditation, like passing by them on the street. It is not at all like sleep. *At times I am aware of slower breathing and reduced heartbeat, sort of a suspended state but not like hypnosis. It is a tremendously unique and very personal experience, you just don't go out and rave about it to your friends. It is almost sacred but not religious at all* [author's italics]. I have more energy,

more determination, and really enjoy my every moment. I guess I am not aware at all of the meditation or of anything going on around me. I usually can't recall any memory of the meditation itself. I can meditate in front of the TV and not hear it at all. It is a very special part of my life. I hope to do it for the rest of my life but I don't promote it because I feel people will find it when they are ready for it.

In answer to the next question on my form, "Have you gotten or can you get this kind of mental experience, which seems to be a typical uniquely pleasurable PA-state experience, in any other way besides meditation," she puts three *X*'s after no, and then says:

Not from religion, sex, childbirth, drugs, illness or hypnosis. It is totally unlike concentration or contemplation. It has never made me feel down, sometimes it makes me feel up but usually just really content and self-confident. It is better than any brief encounter, sensitivity, etc., group because it is ongoing and always readily available.

Mary Kay goes on to say that she elected to meditate after listening to many introductory lectures. She started with some uncertainty but felt that it would be beneficial with some serious problems in her life that were overwhelming her. She meditates for about twenty to sixty minutes once a day between three and five times a week. To my question "How often do you reach what you believe is a deep state of meditation?" she responds, "100 percent of the time." This, of course, is a very subjective question, but most of the meditators who claim that they reach this deep state of meditation also describe reaching the PA state of mind. She, for reasons unknown, has the rare ability to reach the PA state easily through meditation, which may explain why she doesn't feel the need to meditate every day. Every person who experiences it seems to have an amount of the PA state that is sufficient, and evidently what Mary Kay experiences is sufficient for her on a regular but not everyday basis. In response to the question "Have you received any benefit from it, physical or mental?" she states: "It has relaxed me tremendously, helped me to see more humor in life. I am at times intensely aware of colors or shapes that I have seen a million times but never noticed. I have a busier life than before but always feel much calmer and much more in control."

To "Has meditation helped you to get over any bad habit like smoking, drinking, drugs, overeating or gambling?" she responds: "I never drank a lot but now I have very little desire to drink at all; sometimes I can't finish one drink. I don't feel the need for that high or means of relaxing. I eat the same as before but after meditating I am very hungry."

Increased appetite after meditation is a response that many people have reported. It doesn't seem to be anything particularly to worry about because none of them reports that meditation has caused a gain in weight. Some, but not many, have stated it has helped them control their weight, although this is not nearly as common an occurrence with meditation as it is with running. No one who runs ten miles a day is going to be fat.

As I continue here with the responses of other meditators, I will not describe the kind of meditation they practice because I have not found any correlation between what people report and what they practice. Almost all of them have reported greatly diminished use of alcohol; many have stopped drinking, smoking, and the use of drugs altogether.

Patrick Quinn, a twenty-three-year-old psychiatric technician, has been meditating for three years. He started because he suffered from depression and was very unhappy. He meditates twice a day and says he reaches a state of deep meditation about 85 percent of the time. If he doesn't meditate he is uncomfortable, but like many other of the meditators, he describes the discomfort as much milder than that experienced by runners. Most meditators report a mild discomfort, a feeling of missing something valuable, a little tension or guilt, rarely more. Quinn states that meditation has given him a great deal of self-improvement, not so much with his grades, which he says are always good, but with his ability to "write lucid, concise, clear papers and reports." Like many people who have meditated, he states in answer to the question "Have you gotten over any bad habits?": "I have decreased my consumption of mild drugs from daily to occasional use. I have eliminated use of all hallucinatory stimulants and downer drugs."

Patrick's mental experiences while he meditates are similar to many of the others in that he has a no-thought period and when thoughts come he expels them by returning to the mantra; but once in a while, though not enough to be addicting, he reaches the PA state, of which he says: "Occasionally I experience imagery that is so clear and deep I can describe it only as cosmic."

H. Wayne Bradford, a twenty-six-year-old student who has been meditating for four years, says that meditation has helped him a great deal but he still has a long way to go. He says that he had a stiff neck for about eight years and "remembering back to the way it was, it isn't nearly as bad." Commenting on getting over bad habits, he says: "I haven't smoked for over three years. Drinking is down to about one bottle of wine every six months. I will never quit my wine. I stopped using drugs after adding wine to my social activity for five years."

His response to what goes on in his head is:

Sometimes, at least once a week, I experience a feeling of being very large and clear thinking. Large in a free feeling sense of the word, I guess occupying more space than I usually feel . . . this large experience is a feeling that I am without my body but knowing that I am actually inside it but just not feeling it. Then sometimes, very seldom but it has happened a few times, I get a glimpse of a total limitlessness which is very refreshing, more so than the large feeling, which is a rested feeling of contentment.

Again, mostly the pre-PA experience but on occasion the PA state. In answer to the question "Have you ever gotten this in any other way besides meditation?" he says no, and then says of the occasional PA-state experience: "I never dreamed of such a feeling. Drugs, LSD or any other, certainly didn't introduce such an experience. One is too busy being occupied [with drugs] with the outer field of experience and thought."

As with the runners, I have many of these PA-state descriptions, probably at least 75 out of the 700-plus meditators' questionnaires that I received, but almost none of those who report it experience it with the frequency of the runners. From both groups I have quoted the people who are the most articulate, but this does not mean that I am selecting those who have the most frequent or the most profound PA-state experiences. Probably many who meditate and get into the PA state regularly either can't or won't describe what happens. For those who can't, it is *just the experience* that counts. Even if it cannot be described, it nevertheless could be the pure, spinning-free PA state. Those who won't put things into words do not wish to risk losing what they have gained and are perhaps right in following their teachers, all of whom warn them not even to try to put into words what is going on in their heads. To attempt to report what they experience could lead to paying attention, which would block the occurrence of this fragile state. It seems to me, however, that since so many people were able to respond, this indicates that even more could have if they were not inhibited by what I have just described. We can, however, extrapolate from what we have, knowing that the percentage of successful meditators must be higher than the approximately 10 percent who, by their description of their meditation experience, seem to be in the PA state long enough and regularly enough to reach addiction. Robert Winquist, a trusted personal friend who also is a very experienced teacher of TM, confirms that the figure of 10 percent is probably correct. However, the responses of the over one thousand meditators that he has personally instructed and checked show that about 80 percent of them report brief flashes (sometimes no more than a second) of what he would agree is the PA state. He has every reason to believe that this recurs and perhaps increases as they continue to meditate. Though they may never become addicted, it is these momentary PA-state experiences that, both he and I believe, keep them going and give them greater strength.

To reinforce the idea that individuals who meditate should not introspect, I agree completely with the Maharishi and other teachers of this art that if you wish to gain the benefits, it is more important to establish the correct procedures that may lead you to the PA state than it is to attempt to understand what goes on in your head. Nevertheless, as I have said, I don't believe that my respondents have hurt themselves, and their answers are helpful to those who wish to start. To give more indication of the kinds of responses I received, I will quote further from some of the more articulate respondents. I must, however, caution anyone who is meditating now or who wishes to start that this is a purely subjective and individual experience. It is in no way a reflection of your success or failure that you either reach or don't reach what the meditators describe in this chapter. Some typical excerpts from their questionnaires follow:

> Sometimes I space out and feel like I am inside my brain, like it is growing and my brain is all of me, no arms or legs.

> In retrospect I realize that I used to have a great many headaches so I rarely thought about them. Now I hardly ever have one and I frequently wake up euphoric in the morning as if something wonderful is in store but I can't quite remember what it is.

> When I miss meditation it is the same sort of feeling if you don't brush your teeth or bathe each day.

> My success is not in the act of meditating. I would have given up that long ago, but there are times in my daily life when I have been caught up in such joy, I am sure I touched the hem of ecstasy. At other times I see the world around me bathed in such colors as defy description. I have known many shadings of highs brought on by stimuli of happy events, sex, general good spirits, alcohol, but never anything like the joy I spoke of. There are times when it is so intense it is almost too much to bear. These times happen very infrequently, yet they are enough to keep me in the practice of meditation, a task I usually am faithful to but find quite difficult.

It is interesting that the last quoted respondent doesn't meditate so much for what happens during the meditation or even for what it ordinarily does to improve her life. She continues because she believes that meditation is the cause of these infrequent but ecstatic or mystical PA-state experiences which to her are so valuable. Many of the meditators, many more than the runners, say they can get the same experience as in meditation when they are in a beautiful natural setting. What they are describing is the pleasant, relaxing, non-self-critical pre-PA state, a very common occurrence but not to be confused with the PA state. A typical comment: "Something in nature can bring this about, an overwhelming sense of being one. A day in the mountains or on the ocean can do the same thing for me."

Some say that religious experiences like prayer and worship bring the feeling. Others describe the experience as similar to that felt in a few minutes right after orgasm. One person says:

> . . . solitary walks at night, occasional spontaneous experiences of heightened spiritual awareness presumably brought on by a mood of receptiveness to the same. I had a number of drug-induced spiritual experiences five or six years ago but haven't employed that medium since then. Being alone in an outdoor nature setting has also done it.

Another person says he gets an experience similar to meditation:

> Anytime I have an experience which combines the following features—involvement, a sense, conscious or unconscious, of well-being, nondirectional movement, and openness. For me experiencing a sunset or sunrise, a beautiful scene or particularly sailing on a fine day, of being the captain, keeping the boat on an even keel but with no direction in particular, is similar to the oneness I mentioned.

Many meditators, probably 20 percent of my respondents, were moderate to heavy users of drugs, usually marijuana and psychedelics. No one reported the use of heroin. The following is typical of what many of them who had used psychedelics report:

[I used] psychedelic drugs years ago, but drugs wear off, the drug experience wears off. Especially the more they are used, the less chance there is of reaching this experience. Whereas with TM the effects are cumulative and also carry over into nonmeditative daily life after meditation itself may have been forgotten.

As with the runners, I have reported the meditators who believe the practice is highly beneficial to them. I am sure some of the questionnaires were from people pushing TM because their responses were almost verbatim from the TM brochures. This doesn't mean they were not truthful, but I decided to throw those out. Even then (and there must have been about one hundred of these) there were still at least another seven hundred who described benefits I have no reason to doubt. Of these seven hundred about seventy-five described reaching the PA state, in words similar to those I have quoted. As I said, however, meditation is beneficial even if you don't reach the PA state. I am not prepared to say what percentage of people it helps grow stronger. What is important is that a lot of people who do it gain strength, as runners do from their addiction, and there is no risk unless you attempt to do it all day long. Unless you are in solitary confinement like Papillon this would be foolish, and I have no reports of anyone being in any way harmed by this practice.

Although I have studied meditation in some detail I still have no idea how to predict who will be helped by it. I can't even say that it is necessary to go to a formal school like those run by the TM organization to learn. There is no doubt that you can succeed in learning to meditate on your own, as did some of my respondents, or through the use of a widely recommended book like Le-

Shan's *How to Meditate.** In the *New York Times Maga-zine,* February 9, 1975, there is a long article on TM by Maggie Scarf, a freelance writer on science. The whole arti-cle ("Tuning Down with TM") is worth reading, but on the subject of how to learn to meditate she describes the work of a Harvard Medical School cardiologist, Herbert Benson. He has researched the effect of TM on blood pressure and found that as long as it is practiced it does tend to lower the blood pressure of hypertensives, but not to what he would describe as curative levels. Benson took issue with some of the rigid TM practices, especially the secret mantra, and set up his own rules, which are about the same as TM's except he uses the word "one" said with each breath as a mantra. He claims that what he advocates works as well and costs nothing. I don't know. It is tempting to believe that the secrecy of the mantra and the fruit-and-flower ritual is not necessary but it has been used for thousands of years and may have more value than a transient observer like me is able or willing to see.

LeShan, however, who claims to be an expert, has several warnings which seem to me sensible to keep in mind if you are interested in learning to meditate. He says:

> Teachers [of meditation] abound today, some compe-tent, some frauds. You can generally tell a fraud by certain signs. . . . If he is on a "guru" trip and says in effect "follow and obey me without thought or question and I will lead you to enlightenments." If he is running his teaching like a big business. If he says his is the only system that works, walk rapidly to the nearest exit. If he imparts "secret information you must tell no one" he probably belongs in this category as well. Most impor-tantly a teacher should be judged according to what

*Lawrence LeShan, *How to Meditate* (Little Brown, 1974).

kind of a person he is. If his system works to help the student grow in desired directions and if the teacher knows the system well enough to teach it, it should have had an effect upon him [the teacher]. Unless he or she is the kind of person and has the kind of human relationship one respects and admires it is wise to look elsewhere.

Obviously, some of what he says would tend to label TM as a fraud but I don't think he means to do this. I am sure he may have reservations because it is a big business and it does have a tiny, one-time ritual and a secret mantra, but most important from the standpoint of fraudulence, there is no attempt to overcharge the student or intrude upon his life. To the contrary, there is every attempt to follow the student and help him almost indefinitely at no added cost beyond the initial fee. Following LeShan, what I would be careful of is any attempt to get the learner into a cult, a religion, a mystique, or into a deep financial drain. Most important, I believe, is what he says about the teacher. He should be the kind of person who makes you believe that what he practices seems to have had some good effect upon *him*. As in psychiatry, the blind cannot lead the blind. If you go to anyone for help with your life, be he a guru or a counselor, he should be someone whom you easily understand, with whom you can establish mutual respect and confidence, and most of all, whom you like and who you believe likes you.

seven

POSITIVE ADDICTION IN YOUR LIFE

If you believe the PA state is as good as I have described, you won't be surprised if you are seriously considering a regular morning run, a daily period of meditation, or a session of yoga. You may elect to follow the six criteria of Chapter Four and try to find a PA of your own, and if you persist it is possible you will succeed. The key is to persist. It takes considerable self-discipline to become positively addicted, and there is no doubt that the stronger you are the more chance you have, but PA is by no means exclusive to the strong. My inquiries into running and meditating show that many people who lacked confidence or had troublesome symptoms, and even some people with moderate negative addictions, were able to improve their lives considerably through PA. Therefore, while PA takes strength, even an alcoholic or drug addict may have more strength than he believes. If he can begin to experience the non-self-critical relaxation and then momentary flashes of the PA state, this may be enough to keep him going. Besides, being weak does not mean being stupid. Almost all those who suffer from symptoms and most of those who are negatively addicted recognize how much better their lives would be if they were stronger. Since they lack the confidence to get involved with people they could find

PA an attractive alternative because it bypasses this obstacle to their gaining strength. The monk who chanted away his lonely alcoholism is now very much involved with others but his PA gave him the strength to get started. The answers to my questionnaires support this point countless times, but even so, I don't claim that PA is a cure-all for human weakness. *But it is something anyone can try for. There is no risk. Since all positive addictions are simple activities that can be easily accomplished there is no possibility of failure in what you attempt to do. What is hard is to do them long enough to become addicted, but if you quit you are no worse off for having tried.* Therefore, I strongly suggest that anyone, from the weakest negative addict to the strongest among us, consider PA as a way to gain strength. We need all the strength we can get; none of us has a surplus supply.

Truthfully, what makes PA so attractive for the weak and lonely, that they can do it on their own, is for many others a shortcoming, because not only can you do it on your own; you *must* do it on your own. It is not a social thing. There are no classes, groups, or programs that can do any more than get you started. After that it is up to you. Therefore, for many fairly strong people, most of whom are not used to doing things alone and who are obviously not driven by the pain of weakness, PA may be hard to reach. You will recall it took Joe Henderson, a dedicated runner, two years to reach PA but in fairness it must be mentioned he was competing at the time. Meditating takes less time but as explained in Chapter Six the percentage of meditators who reach addiction is low, maybe only 10 percent. The other positive addictions fall somewhere in between the hard physical activity of running and the attempt at total physical and mental inactivity that is good meditation, but even to be effortless takes more practice than most of us are willing to expend. Therefore, the PA state is beyond the reach of most adults unless we are willing to make a great deal of effort for at least an hour almost every day. This is unfortunate because early in our lives, usually in the preschool years from two to five, the PA state occurs naturally. Watch a small child playing by himself in a sandbox or with a little car, a few stones, or a doll, and you will see episodes of repetitive, almost trancelike pauses in play. They seem to occur naturally, last for anywhere from a few seconds to several minutes, and then the child returns to more vigorous activity. Where he may have been almost automatically moving the toy car, or sifting sand, or smoothing the doll's hair or dress, he now engages in active play as he comes out of his brief but natural PA state. As he grows, however, especially when he enters school, he is able to have these moments less and less. He is bombarded too much with the standard admonitions of our culture. He is told to stop daydreaming, get on the ball, not to waste time, to buckle down, all of which tell him the payoff is to pay attention and keep his mind occupied. He soon learns to abort these natural PA-state experiences and once he gets the knack of preventing their occurrence, a knack almost all of us develop at an early age, he successfully stops them for good. One way to recapture them as an adult is to develop a positive addiction. This is the only way most of us can overcome the barrier of self-criticism that our culture has inculcated into all of us, a barrier that keeps the PA state away. Occasionally, however, the PA state does break through naturally when we are adults. Greeley and McCready, in the research reported in Chapter Three, found about 40 percent of all adults have had one such experience; 20 percent said it has occurred several times; and 5 percent have it often but do not specify what "often" means. I would suspect some but not all of the latter are positive addicts. I would have suspected more of them were if they had said regularly instead of often. When it occurs spontaneously many adults, including the authors of the article, tend to believe that it is religious in origin. This helps them explain these PA-state experiences—it's a traditional way of looking at them; otherwise they would worry that this euphoric happening is crazy. Not only is it not crazy, but, as reported in Chapter Three, it seems to correlate higher with mental well-being on a valid psychological test than anything else yet discovered. It is, however, part of our self-critical mores that we are taught early to regard this natural occurrence of the PA state as abnormal and to keep up our guard against it. Most of us do this well; only 5 percent of us are relaxed enough and accepting of ourselves that we can enjoy its benefits naturally.

We do, however, pay a price when we learn to deny ourselves this naturally strengthening phenomenon. Part of the price is losing a chance to grow stronger, another part is keeping up the vigilance needed to prevent its occurrence. This vigilance becomes built in very early, probably soon after we start school, and in most of us it is successful in preventing the natural PA state. Being constantly on guard takes energy; it adds a constant low level of tension to our already tense lives. Then, if we aren't too successful in finding love and worth, I believe that many of us, starting as early as our teens in an effort to break this tension, become negatively addicted. We substitute a brief but sure, chemically induced PA state to get the relaxation we so desperately need. The drugs are usually mild like caffeine or nicotine but they work because they induce regular but momentary flashes of the PA state which partially make up for what, as children, we experienced naturally. People drinking coffee, usually with a cigarette, use these drugs not only for their minimal pain-reducing qualities but also for the moment of brain relaxation their use affords. Without the coffee, cola, and cigarette "break" many people believe they couldn't make it through the day. Unfortunately, the more we use drugs, even drugs as mild as caffeine or nicotine, the more we become used to the drug-induced pleasure and the more we depend upon these chemicals for regular relaxation. We soon become addicted, as perhaps half the adults in this country are, to coffee and cigarettes. This addiction, mild as it is, effectively blocks any chance whatsoever for the natural process to break through. As in all chemical addictions, when the caffeine or nicotine wears off we are quickly back to where we were and in addition have the added pain of withdrawal. Caffeine and nicotine are not serious addictions—at best they provide only flashes of the PA state—but they are harmful because they interfere with our ability to relax naturally. The more we smoke the more tense we get when we are not smoking, but since smoking is the main way to break the tension we are caught in a vicious circle. A positive addiction is often reported as a way to break this circle by allowing us enough of the natural PA state to become strong enough to relax sufficiently and no longer have to smoke. Many of those who reach PA regularly report that drinking and drug use are no longer necessary. It is my belief that chemicals even as mild as nicotine and caffeine chemically deny us mental strength and may also block the creative process. Because they seem to provide relaxation they may give us the illusion of strength but that's all. It might be argued that many creative people smoke, drink coffee, and even use drugs, but this in no way shows that they need these drugs to be creative. If they could gain the strength to stop these mild or severe chemical assaults on their brains, they might be even more creative. If, however, they are very weak, as are some creative people who have many symptoms, then maybe these mild addictions do help, for without them they would be too tense to do anything. The same might be said of alcohol and tranquilizers, but the more addicted a person is to strong drugs, the less creative he will be. In fact, there used to be an old psychiatric myth that to be artistic or creative you needed to be neurotic (weak) and that good therapy could endanger the creative impulse. Nothing could be farther from the truth. Creativity is intimately tied to strength not weakness. It may be that with newfound strength some suffering artists may take the time to enjoy some long overdue love and friendship, which may slow them down artistically for a while. But when their need for love is satisfied they soon pick up and are usually much more productive and creative than before. In life, two negatives don't make a positive, and those who are strong and don't rely on drugs are always better off.

To show how far we have gone in accepting both tension and addiction and denying the value of natural, nonchemical relaxation, I would like to cite from an article in one of the throw-away magazines I recently read on an airliner. In it were listed the responses of company managers to the suggestion that their employees be allowed to meditate for twenty minutes in place of a coffee break. Most of them scoffed at it and many said it was a dangerous suggestion. They didn't want their employees to relax. They said it was good for them to be tense, to be worried, to be tight. It made them better workers and better competitors. Almost to a man they believed that relaxation is the enemy of competition and productivity. To judge from the data I have gathered here this common belief is dead wrong. If employees who wished to do so were allowed a short time to meditate, even if they didn't reach the PA state, they would be stronger, more resilient, and more creative. They would also be appreciative of the fact that the company allowed them this benefit and they would naturally use much of the strength gained on company time for the company's benefit. Companies that discover this, however, may then mistakenly choose to make meditation company policy, thus destroying its benefits for most of their employees because it has to be voluntary or it won't work. It can't be forced upon anyone.

As I was thinking about the responses of these company managers, it occurred to me that maybe this prevalent attitude was similar to that of the old schoolmaster who drilled his pupils rigorously in the classics. He was usually convinced that the nose-to-the-grindstone discipline needed to learn Greek and Latin was excellent preparation for life. To bolster his belief he could cite student after student whose diligent work in this area had paid off in outstanding careers later. He had no proof this was the case but the common wisdom of the time supported him and the classics were the foundation of the traditional curriculum. Today, this belief has been discredited. Students excel without Greek or Latin, but in a way I believe there was some truth to the belief in the value of a classical curriculum. This value, however, was less inherent and more in the fact that the books studied were uniformly boring. As a student fought his way through these tomes in Latin or Greek, it was easy to drift off. They served as a kind of academic mantra providing easy access to the far reaches of the bored student's mind. Reading the Odyssey in Greek produced mental journeys far more strange and wonderful than the wanderings of Odysseus. To be condemned to these works was for young active minds like Papillon being condemned to the dungeon and, like him, as they struggled with their assignments, they regularly drifted off to the PA state. If a student was so unfortunate as to master them by having to keep his nose to the grindstone and never allowing himself to drift, they must have been both excruciating and totally worthless. If, however, you were a good student and had an insightful teacher who graded easily and you managed to pass your courses in the classics, then you got the full PA benefit because you had no need to criticize yourself for failing; in fact, you were probably exultant. I feel the test of a great classic may be that it provide long passages of constructive boredom which, as you study, cause your brain in desperation to spin out regularly.

In sharp contrast, today's child is bombarded with television that is relentlessly stimulating to his immature mind. Television, whether it is children's programs or not, is created by people who want both the eyes and ears of those who watch it to be completely occupied. This goal is unfortunately reached almost 100 percent in children under ten, much less so in older children and adults. The commercials are especially jarring and attention getting, and in the programs violence is piled on violence, keeping the child continually stimulated. This excessive stimulation has an insidiously destructive effect on the young because it prevents them from drifting off into their natural PA state. A child needs these natural PA-state experiences. They are calming and strengthening, but if he is in front of the TV eight hours a day (average for preschool children) there is little chance they will occur.

In *The Identity Society,* I explained that TV also interferes with children socializing. When they should be actively playing they are passively watching TV, and they later go to school drastically deficient in the social skills. Finally there is the violence, the antisocial stimulation that leads them in their weakened state to try acting out themselves to see if they can get the same kicks personally that they see so many people "enjoy" on the TV. Thus TV deprives them of love and worth by interfering with the time they need to socialize, play, and learn, and it also deprives them of their natural PA state, both of which reduce their strength. Therefore, weak because TV has interfered with both the active and passive paths to strength, when they are faced with the mild stress of school many choose to give up or act out. The present epidemic of hyperactive children is a symptomatic acting-out reaction because they haven't the strength to stand the ordinary routine of school. They find difficulty partly because they are too weak to concentrate and partly because school routine does not cater to their social need for constant gratification, as does TV. If children are not helped to grow stronger through a social and thoughtful education, where their acting out is handled with toughness and where stimulating choices are a part of the curriculum, they fail in school, they become delinquent, and the whole sordid picture of juvenile problems unfolds. While TV affects all children adversely it is lower-economic-class children, especially those of minority groups, who are most harmed because they have the fewest alternatives to TV and watch it most. Thus TV is a major force in keeping the impoverished children weak and inadequate and in doing so it locks them into poverty. To escape from their economic class they need as much strength as, if not more than, the middle-class children with whom they are forced to compete.

We need strong public education programs, privately sponsored (the government is craven here), to tell all parents to ration the amount of TV their children watch, maybe an hour a day for preschool, two hours for children up to eleven. After eleven they watch it less and it is before eleven that most of the damage is done. Here some readers will say I am using TV as a whipping boy; parental ineffectiveness and social discrimination are far more important. Even if they are right—and I don't think they are—the fact is that we can reduce TV viewing far more easily than we can make families stay together and end social discrimination. Whether TV is the major factor or not, less TV will produce stronger children. To me it is not a question of who is right but a question of what can be done. I believe, given this information, many parents would respond, although the stronger the parent the more likely he is to make the effort to limit TV.

Another suggestion that I now make to educators is to allow fifteen minutes a day in elementary school for each child (and maybe each teacher) to do his or her own thing. The child can do anything at all as long as he chooses it, as long as it is possible to do in school or on the playground, and as long as he can do it by himself and not interfere with anyone else. My purpose is to try to set up a time for each child (and teacher) to engage in non-self-critical activity. Students and teachers won't get into the PA state, but even a short time in a totally self-accepting activity will give them better access to their own minds. Emerson Hough School in Newton, Iowa, now doing this as an experiment, believes that it does have a beneficial effect. It needs to be explained and worked out but it could provide a needed dimension of freedom to our overprogrammed schools.

In between the positive addictions and the rare naturally occurring PA state are a group of pleasurable activities where drifting off usually occurs as part of the activity. These activities are not addictions but we enjoy them and they are a valuable means of adding to our strength. As I said earlier, maybe they are to PA as binges are to negative addictions. Examples of these activities are fishing, hunting, climbing, walking, driving for pleasure, bird watching or whale watching, sunbathing, sitting on the beach and watching the waves, or watching a fire crackle up a chimney. All of these activities bring a contentment and peace that are unique to them and they are all possible entrees to an occasional PA-state experience. I personally have fished alone for hours, caught next to nothing, yet on a calm, warm, pleasant summer afternoon have had the time fly by. Suddenly the day was gone and it was night. The whole experience was so pleasant that I am sure it was interspersed with occasional episodes of the PA state between the even more occasional fish. That the PA state is at times experienced in nature is one of the great attractions of viewing the waves, a sunset, some mountains, or walking through the woods. When it is mutually experienced, as sometimes occurs, it can bring people closer to themselves and to each other than almost any other way.

I believe, therefore, that we should program our children and ourselves less completely than we do. We should allow for time off, some leeway, some slack in the day; never make it too tight. Even in the army, miserable and programmed as it was, I learned the value of waiting, especially waiting in line. During the totally organized and frenetically active basic training, waiting in line for me was an oasis, a place where I could drift on my own, where I could take time to renew my head. For many soldiers waiting in line was an agony of boredom. Instead of relaxing and drifting off they resented the army's inefficiency in having lines everywhere. Maybe the army knew more than they did. Maybe we needed this time. I know I did. I wasn't conditioned to believe that in the army or anywhere else there wasn't some value in a little wasted time.

Again, I am sure I will be misunderstood and perhaps condemned by some readers as deviating in this book from the no-nonsense Reality Therapy in which for years I have stressed action: face reality, solve problems, get involved, and get it done. In my defense, I would like to explain that I am not deviating at all. I still believe completely that we should face reality, but I have found in Reality Therapy that the client needs to gain strength to accomplish his plans. Much of that strength, of course, comes from his involvement with the therapist. The crux of this involvement, however, is the quiet acceptance that he should enjoy with a good therapist. For many people who have symptoms and seek help, this short period each week with an accepting therapist may be the only time in years they have had this kind of acceptance. This does not mean blanket acceptance of the client by the therapist regardless of what he does. It is an acceptance which is always conditional; the condition is he begin to face his problems and make plans to solve them. How much and how quickly to enforce this condition is part of the technique of therapy, which is beyond the scope of this book. If the therapist is skilled, however, he can convince most clients that this condition is so obviously to their benefit that it does not interfere with the acceptance that helps them to get deeper into their own minds where there is strength. Some clients report that they get help by sitting in the reception room, waiting to see me or my associates. What they are saying is that the waiting room itself becomes a haven in which they can accept themselves. So while I believe in the importance of getting down to brass tacks and making plans, it has been my experience that you can make plans until hell freezes over but if you haven't the ability to produce a reasonably non-self-critical therapeutic milieu the client won't have the strength to carry the plans out. If to this therapeutic atmosphere the client can also add some regular time in the PA state on his own, the resulting increase in strength may help him turn the tide in his favor. Although I now have a very small practice, I have recently suggested meditation to an extremely tense client and running to a client who is overweight. It will be interesting to see if the combination of good therapy plus PA works. A San Diego psychiatrist, Dr. Thaddeus L. Kostrubala, who has been recommending running to all of his patients who will give it a try, says he does not understand why running helps mental well-being, "but I have never had such a breakthrough in medical knowledge in my whole life." As he sees patients in his practice improve through running he goes on to say, "I am intrigued beyond belief by what I am seeing happen."*

In every society there seems to be some balance, some amount of time that one needs to be in the PA state to lead the most fulfilled life. In our society and our culture, this time appears to be no more than an hour a day and probably a lot less is sufficient. The only way most of us, weak or strong, can come even close to getting this on a regular basis is to become positively addicted. Maybe the time will come when we will learn to treat our children and each other noncritically enough so that the PA state will return naturally. I don't foresee this in the predictable future but I am in hopes that this book will stimulate people to attempt PA. At the risk of being repetitious, I must again warn that it is not easy to become positively addicted. If you wish to try, be persistent and you may be more than pleasantly surprised by what happens in your life if you succeed.

*Lew Scarr, Copley News Service, from an article, "Run for Your Sanity," Redondo *Daily Breeze* (February 10, 1975).

INDEX

Index